On Holiday Again, Doctor?

On Holiday Again, Doctor?

DR ROBERT CLIFFORD

Illustrated by Larry

PELHAM BOOKS

for MARGARET IDDON

who for seven years has patiently typed my manuscripts,
praying each night that one day I am going to surprise her
with a word processor

First published in Great Britain by
Pelham Books Ltd
27 Wrights Lane
London W8 5TZ
1987

British Library Cataloguing in Publication Data
Clifford, Robert
    On holiday again, Doctor?
    1. Medicine, Rural——England——Somerset
    I. Title
    610'.92'4   R488.S6

    ISBN 0-7207-1773-6

Typeset at The Spartan Press Ltd,
Lymington, Hants
Printed and bound by
Billing & Sons Ltd, Worcester

Contents

Prologue

Life is a tragedy, for we are all born eventually to die. We survive our tragedies by laughing at them.

A friend once told me that when he was under the influence of ether he dreamed he was turning over the pages of a great book, in which he knew he would find, on the last page, the meaning of life.

The pages of the book were alternately tragic and comic, and he turned page after page, his excitement growing, not only because he was approaching the answer, but because he couldn't know, until he arrived, on which side of the book the final page would be. At last it came: the universe opened up to him in a hundred words: and they were uproariously funny.

He came back to consciousness crying with laughter, remembering everything. He opened his lips to speak. It was then that the great and comic answer plunged back out of his reach.

Christopher Fry

CHAPTER 1

Back to the Wall

I had my back to the wall.

I literally had my back to the wall. This particular wall being the outside of a Moroccan toilet in the Todra Gorge.

Behind the wall, a very distressed New Zealand girl in a long white nightdress was trying to cope with a severe attack of gastro-enteritis. Her only light source was the matches she struck in the less acute stages of her attack to give her some idea of her footing, which was two precarious mounds in the shape of feet.

If toilets were rated in an amenity range of one to ten, this one would have been given minus one.

On my side of the wall, I was facing three shouting, gesticulating Moroccans who were advancing, intent on doing me some bodily harm.

I'd never known how I would behave with my back to the wall, being threatened by hostile tribesmen. As a youth I had read in the *Hotspur* and the *Wizard* how simple it was: just hit them with a cricket bat.

To my own surprise – I'm not generally a violent man – I was longing for one of them to get near enough to lay my hands on him.

I was just about at the end of my tether and these three gesticulating gentlemen were in danger of making it snap. One of the ingredients of my incipient bravery was the fact that all three of them were much smaller than I was, although had I laid hands on them I would probably have found knives flicking out from every pocket.

They were after my women. When I say *my* women, I was part of a band of 29 travellers, mainly women, supposedly on a conducted camping and hotel tour of Morocco.

The men got closer, screaming: 'Why do you keep the women all to yourself?' My fists clenched in pleasurable anticipation of the first blow. Then I said in my best French: 'It is best if Nameless Tours never visit the Todra Gorge again.' At these magic words my potential attackers immediately changed into drivelling, apologetic men, backing off with a thousand apologies. They were only joking, they had suddenly seen that their action could have involved them in a major loss of income. At this moment my New Zealand girl poked her head round the door and said that she was well enough to return to our room. 'Our room' meant a furnished Oxo cube that would have made the Black Hole of Calcutta look like a four-star hotel.

This was another disastrous day on another disastrous tour. When we got to the Todra Gorge, our guide-driver said there would be no need for us to put up our tents that night. There weren't enough tents to go round anyway, and he'd found us a room which we could all share. He then disappeared with the most striking blonde in the party to some private accommodation, and this was the last we saw of him until the morning. Our room was about the size of a small dining room and 28 of us were expected to spend the night there.

There had been trouble in the evening. We had with us some precocious young Australian and New Zealand girls who were egging the local boys on. As most of the local women went round looking like bell tents with only a small slit for them to look out of, the sight of our scantily clad Australasians was more than they could bear. The fact that they were only being teased made it even worse.

2

There was some vague sort of Moroccan music in the evening, some talk of drugs and then the arrival of the local Chief of Police. We couldn't quite make out what it was he wanted; whether our girls had been taking drugs, I don't know. The girls were now terrified – we had 30 or 40 menacing-looking Moroccans advancing on us – and the whole party looked to me for instruction.

The fact that I was looked to for leadership in the absence of our driver was not that I am a natural leader of men: it was just that I was middle-aged.

My wife Pam feels it does me good to get away into the wild every now and then, so I'd booked for this trip across Morocco. From the brochure, it sounded very similar to the marvellous Sahara trips I'd had, but I found when I got there that the trip was for under 35s. Being 53 at the time gave me some position of seniority.

'Right, everybody,' I said in best boy scout fashion. 'Slowly and casually back towards our room.' We managed to make a steady retreat and shut the door. Some of the girls were whimpering with fright.

'There's nothing to worry about,' I said, although I felt worried sick. 'Just bed down for the night. It'll all look quite different in daylight.'

The door started to open and one of the Moroccan men outside tried to join us. I shut the door firmly on him and sat down leaning against the door, hoping at least to get a little sleep. Being, as usual, overweight, I made a good doorstop to protect the chastity of our women passengers.

All the travellers weren't under 35. Robin Treaton was in fact 47. His contribution to calming the fears of our girls was to take two of the more nubile ones naked into his sleeping bag with him. This might have sounded crowded but the room was so small that this was just about par for the course. He lay in the middle of his bag grinning from ear to ear. 'Not a bad holiday eh, Bob?' he said.

Everybody settled down and I was half-dozing in my sitting position as doorstop when my little New Zealand girl got up

3

from the far side of the room, ran across the sleeping bags and vomited straight over me. 'Quick!' she said. 'I must get to the toilet!'

We opened the door. Outside there were about 30 Moroccans sleeping with blankets or coats wrapped round them. I had to escort her, tiptoeing over the sleeping bodies to the toilet where I had my confrontation with the three violent men. We had no further trouble from the men after my magic words, but the New Zealand girl's condition did not go away. About every 20 minutes she would jump up and I had to escort her through the sleeping throng back to this filthy toilet, which I wouldn't have liked on a good day and, on this particular day, I hated. I had no assistance from any of the other 28 members of my party, some who slept soundly; some, mainly the women, who didn't sleep a wink. Apparently someone in the room asked whether I was all right, facing the mob outside. The questioner was immediately reassured by Robin from his crowded sleeping bag, who shouted, 'Don't worry, he'll be all right.'

At last dawn came. My little New Zealand girl was now almost completely dehydrated, but some of the worst aspects of her symptoms had disappeared. As the room stirred, all modesty was forgotten. Men and women who had been strangers just a few days ago were now intermingled, pulling clothes on, some of the women crying, but all of us welcoming the dawn as it arose.

I opened the door gingerly. All the sleeping Moroccans had gone and there was no sign of the three who had threatened me in the toilet.

Our driver-cum-courier appeared, full of beans, with his blonde companion. He asked if we'd had a good night and was nearly lynched on the spot, while his blonde companion was ostracised by all the other lady members of the party. We were a sorry lot.

Our next night's stop was a camping stop beside a swimming pool. We unloaded the bus, managed to get up enough tents to cover all of us, but it did mean people sharing a single tent. I had a quick dip in the pool, a cup of coffee, two sleeping capsules and slept for 24 hours. I awoke in blinding sunshine to find all the party in bikinis happily chatting away around the pool, with food cooking on some stoves, all as if nothing had happened.

My trip to Morocco was a potential disaster from the beginning. I had done some desert travelling and, knowing how cold it was at night, had taken two sleeping bags. Both were stoutly wrapped in an old tent bag with my name and, as an extra precaution, the tour party's name stencilled on it. I was the epitome of an efficient traveller.

Unfortunately they couldn't find my sleeping bag at Casablanca airport, so I spent the two weeks of the trip using the working sleeping bag of the driver, an oily old bag he used to lie on when working under the bus.

The main problem with this particular expedition was numbers. It was Easter, many of the tour party were schoolteachers on holiday, and we were 29 people in a 29-seater bus. This sounds reasonable, but normally there are only 20 people on each tour. There were only tents and equipment for 20 people, and at least a third of the bus was required to carry equipment, personal belongings, tents and cooking utensils. The tour was supposed to be a mixture of camping and native hotels. We cooked for ourselves as we went along. There was to be some time in a proper hotel in Marrakesh where we were promised beds, baths, showers and everything. I couldn't wait.

As well as the position that I'd assumed as deputy leader of the party, because I was a doctor there was always a morning surgery. Not only had people developed conditions while on the tour, some were wanting advice for problems they'd had for 20 or 30 years. On my first day, a very nice young girl had come up to me asking if I would mind having a look at her legs. She had quite a serious generalised condition called Erythema Nodosum for which she should have been hospitalised straight away (and in fact was immediately on her return from the trip). But once we'd started there was no way back, so we were carrying one really ill person from the very beginning. This girl was an extremely nice lass who made as little as possible of her painful legs and did her best to get something out of this disastrous holiday.

At last the move came to Marrakesh, a beautiful town with one of the biggest casbahs I've ever seen. The only thing that spoilt it was the fact you couldn't walk a yard without being bothered by touts who were offering anything from silk scarves and dresses to their grandmothers. We stayed at the Charles Foucald Hotel: it was extremely comfortable and the food was good. I even managed with one of the Dutch passengers, a very attractive young lady, to have a meal at the Mirimour Hotel, Churchill's favourite watering place in Morocco. Perhaps the holiday wasn't going to be too bad after all.

We were due to leave the hotel on a horseriding trip for three days, but disaster struck again. The number of people and the limitation of the equipment on the bus meant that plates weren't properly washed and hygiene wasn't looked after. After 24 hours in Marrakesh, half of the party were down with severe gastro-enteritis, at least as severe as the little New Zealand girl, who was now fit enough to join in all activities. Not so a dozen of

6

the other passengers who were far too ill to leave the hotel. As all in the party were much younger than I, and had been brought up on the National Health, they assumed that it was quite normal for me to stay and look after them. Robin Treaton acted as a runner for me, going to the pharmacist with prescriptions, and coming back with bags of charcoal and various medications.

One girl was in hysterics because her boyfriend had gone off on the riding trip, leaving her ill in the hotel. That was the end of at least one of the many partnerships in our group.

I'd come well prepared for any medical eventuality but hadn't thought I'd be looking after nearly 30 people. We just about managed until I went down with the gripes myself, having it as bad as most or even worse. I did find a secluded room for myself to endure my illness in private.

I had been sharing a room with Robin Treaton, but felt I was cramping his style. Unfortunately for him our double room was marked as the Doctors' Room. The first day that I was in isolation, Robin who didn't know an aspirin from an enema but was assumed by the hotel staff to have some sort of medical qualification was dragged protesting to the room to see the hysterical girl whose boyfriend had gone off on the riding trip.

The staff forced their way into her room to find that her gastro-enteritis had been so acute that the carpet was showing signs that she had not always made it to the communal toilet. To find that Robin had been forcibly propelled into her room in its dishevelled state as her medical adviser, was too much for the poor girl. She collapsed on the bed, screaming at the top of her voice. The management and Robin fled, leaving the mess for the boyfriend to clear up when he came back.

Somehow we survived our two weeks. We went to Agadir, we went up into the Atlas mountains. It was all a bit of a blur. We saw the mud fort where Lawrence of Arabia had made part of some film, but it couldn't have been Lawrence of Arabia, it must have been Peter O'Toole . . . I was becoming disorientated. Yes, I remember: it was another night when our guide-driver announced that instead of tents he had triumphantly found us another of his Black Holes of Calcutta. On this occasion there were no marauding Moroccans in the toilet. I think our young girls had learnt their lesson.

The plane home was delayed for ten hours at Casablanca airport. When I arrived at the airport, having spent a fortnight in an oily, cold sleeping bag, I was greeted by a smiling official with my two sleeping bags done up in their beautifully numbered tent bag. Then to my great surprise, just as the plane was about to leave, all the other passengers gathered in a group. A spokesman came forward to say how much they'd appreciated the great care I had taken of them during the stay, and there, as a present from all my sick passenger patients, was a Moroccan silver bowl. I almost wept.

The silver bowl is now on my mantlepiece as a reminder never to go to Morocco again, at least not with Nameless Tours at Easter.

CHAPTER 2

A Town Like Tadchester

I am not really an experienced and intrepid world traveller, but the fourth partner in a group of five and a half partners in general practice in a little Somerset town called Tadchester. Tadchester is a market town with a rising population of about 8,000. It stands on the estuary of the River Tad in one of the most beautiful parts of the Somerset coast, with the resorts of Sandford-on-Sea and Stowin nearby. Although primarily a market town, it still has some fishing, an increasing amount of light industry and a small mine that produces pigments, a residue from the time when the main industry of the town was coal-mining.

In Tadchester you're not just a Tadchester resident, you are either strictly Up-the-Hill or Down-the-Hill. The town is split by the river, with high ground on one side that leads eventually down to the coastal resort of Stowin, and flat ground on the other side which was presumably marshland in years gone by and which has been reclaimed. The river goes down to the sea, passing the shipbuilding yard of Peargate, round the corner from which is the other seaside resort of Sandford-on-Sea. This physical division by the river means that you are either an Up-the-Hill or a Down-the-Hill person.

In the past this had important social distinctions. The

9

population of Up-the-Hill tended to be the have-nots, whereas Down-the-Hill they tended to be the haves. It has levelled off over the years with the coming of light industry which was mainly Up-the-Hill. Now, although there are no social distinctions between the halves of the town, there is no lessening of the rivalry.

We were the only general practice in the town and also took care of the local hospital. Of the five full partners, each had his own area of responsibility in the hospital. Steve Maxwell, the senior partner had a special interest in medicine, Henry Johnson the second senior was the surgeon, Jack Hart the third partner was the anaesthetist. I, the fourth partner, was reckoned to be an expert in midwifery, although in the more recent years this meant just sending expectant mothers to the new midwifery hospital at Winchcombe.

Our fifth partner was Ron Dickinson, an accomplished athlete who spent a great deal of his time running, jumping, swimming, sailing, water skiing and removing the local tonsils. Our half-partner was Catherine Carlton, the delightful wife of a dentist, who was a much nicer doctor than all of us. Catherine gave the proper balance to the practice and was always available for ladies to come and talk to about things ladies prefer to discuss only with other ladies. We were a happy and well-balanced team, living in a delightful area.

One of the reasons I had moved to Tadchester in the first place, apart from the fact that I liked the partners and the partnership, was because it was in a lovely holiday area. I felt that living near the seaside would mean that at holiday time I wouldn't have to travel very far. However, I'd only been in practice for a few months before my appearance on the beach meant that an impromptu surgery would shortly assemble.

No matter how secluded the bay, eventually patients would track me down, and before very long there were few local places I could visit for relaxation or refreshment. A patient on the beach with a few drinks inside him was often much less inhibited than he was in the surgery, and much more difficult to get rid of.

It had long been my ambition to have a holiday at home where I could get stuck into the garden and do odd things around the house, but whenever I had time off at home news would flash round the grapevine that I wasn't at the surgery. People would drop in with: 'I know you're on holiday, but you're the only one that understands Grandma. I won't take a minute of your time.' Which meant taking an hour of my time.

Once while moving house I was walking along the street with a chest of drawers on my shoulder, when I was stopped and asked if I was on duty. 'No,' I replied. 'I'm off sick with a chest complaint.' And I staggered on with my mighty load. My questioner looked puzzled.

It's not always appreciated how onerous the working hours of general practitioners are. When I started in general practice I attended an average of three home confinements a fortnight. I was on every other week for emergency anaesthetics for the hospital, apart from all other practice commitments and emergencies. It was not uncommon to miss a whole night's sleep and have to work the next day. Sometimes all the partners would be together at night, operating on some vital case, and still have to appear the next day.

Once I missed two whole nights' sleep running and continued working. But on the third day of this marathon I went out on a visit, came to a crossroads – and forgot which side of the road one drove on. If doctors were airline pilots or even lorry drivers, we wouldn't be allowed to work these hours. It's one of the quirks of our society that there's no restriction on the hours worked by a man whose job, ostensibly, is to keep people alive.

Holidays are important for everyone, and doctors in particular. Doctors, alas, must get away from their home base, otherwise the holiday just becomes an extension of their work. Most doctors take six weeks' holiday a year. On the other hand they probably work, as I did, 17 to 20 weekends a year, most public holidays and every Christmas. I worked out that if I had every weekend and bank holiday off, plus just a fortnight's holiday, I would actually have more time than I did with the six precious weeks that I took away from the practice.

With the enlightened partners with whom I worked it was agreed that every seven years we should take 13 weeks off to go and do our own thing; anything from working in a mission hospital in India to lying in the sun in Italy. Thus, although it would appear that I and my family have taken lots and lots of holidays everywhere, as we obviously have done, many of them I would have swapped for a quiet undisturbed week's pottering about the house.

Many patients think that their doctors are continually on holiday. I can see a patient 30 times in one year, but if I happen to be away on the 31st occasion he visits the surgery, I'm accused of letting him down and never being there when he needs me. Whenever I announce I'm about to take some well-earned break – which usually means rushing around working twice as hard both before the holiday and for the first week I'm back – there are always raised eyebrows from my quite bewildered patients.

Speaking in chorus they say: 'What? On holiday again, Doctor?'

CHAPTER 3

In Transit

One of my close friends was Chris Parfitt, Editor of the *Tadchester Gazette*, known to everyone as C. P. I thought it would be a great idea for him and his family to join the Clifford clan on a fortnight's holiday in France.

C. P. was reluctant at first. He'd known several longstanding friendships break up during family holidays together. And he wasn't too keen on Abroad *per se*, after one or two unfortunate experiences out there.

His National Service in the Sudan had put him off strong sunshine for life. In transit in Malta he was narrowly missed by a shotgun blast, aimed by a local farmer who was peeved about previous damage done by British squaddies to his drystone walls.

On a family holiday in Spain, the hotel was crammed with overweight Germans who commandeered the swimming pool every day for mass bellyflop sessions. And he made the mistake of watching a bullfight in Barcelona. A young matador botched one of the kills and C. P. left the bullring feeling sick.

In Tangier he'd been horrified by the stumps of arms shoved under his nose by mutilated child beggars, and by the sight of a suspected petty thief being hauled screaming into the local police station for what promised to be a horrendous beating-up.

In Italy he'd been put off his cannelloni at a pavement cafe by the sight of a starving and mange-ridden cat hobbling painfully across the road.

Even in Gibraltar he didn't have the luck. One morning the hotel bar provided lashings of *tapas* – crispy bits of fried fish provided free with the drinks. They were delicious and C. P. ate his fill.

Next day, when he'd recovered from an all-night bout of food poisoning, he discovered that the fish were horse mackerel. Not only that, they'd been collected from a dry dock which had been drained to service a British aircraft carrier. The horse mackerel had been eating all the waste discharged from the ship, richly supplemented by the throwing-up of the sailors returned from a night on the town.

'So all in all, Bob, you could say I'm not one hundred per cent keen on the idea,' he said. 'Apart from anything else, you can't get a decent pint.'

C. P. had the journalist's occupational liking for a pint of beer, and treated the drinking of one with reverence. A badly kept or sloppily served pint – even worse, a pint of keg beer – was to him the equivalent of breaking wind in church.

Eventually, however, he agreed to put it to a family council. His wife Joyce and their children, Clive and Janet, were wholeheartedly in favour. Democracy prevailed by a vote of three to one.

We got down to the planning – Pam and myself, our two younger children Paul and Jane, and the Parfitts – for a fortnight in France. We'd decided to travel in a Ford Transit van and work our way down to the Dordogne: camping a few nights, staying *en pension* a few nights, and finishing up for a week in a villa I'd booked.

I'd seen the villa advertised in a medical magazine. It was expensive, but it was set in magnificent Dordogne countryside and sounded luxurious.

With all our luggage and camping gear, the van was full to

15

bursting. A tentative suggestion from C. P. that we might find room for a barrel of Barnsley Best Bitter to tide him over until he got used to the filthy French muck, was outvoted.

'Perhaps as well,' he said. 'Temperamental stuff, that. Doesn't travel well.'

We decided to go by hovercraft, taking the cheapest route from Dover to Calais, forgetting that we'd have to drive to Dover, and that we'd have an extra day's travelling through France before we got anywhere near the Dordogne.

The hovercraft sailed at about eleven in the morning, so it meant a chilly dawn start. I had a few twinges of regret on the journey toward Dover as we passed Southampton and Portsmouth, where we could easily have taken ferries to Cherbourg or Le Havre.

Somewhere near Guildford in Surrey, the holiday began with breakfast at a Happy Eater.

'Last bacon and eggs for a bit,' muttered C. P. 'May as well make the most of it.'

We arrived at Dover with time to spare. Knowing how bad we all were at handling money, we decided to buy all our duty-free liquor there and carry it round with us. It would mean that, even if we overspent in France, we would still have something to show for it at the end of the holiday.

In 40 minutes we had crossed the Channel. There's always a tremendous excitement about landing in France: the thrill of putting the Channel behind you, of seeing your first gendarme, of driving on the other side of the road and hoping you won't make a mess of negotiating the junctions.

I had elected to do all the driving. C. P. did not get on too well with the horseless carriage, and admitted to being the worse driver in the world. Even had he claimed to be the best, his family would soon have put the record straight.

We had a leisurely drive south for about 200 miles to our first campsite. It was leisurely mainly because the heavily laden van was reluctant to go above 50 miles an hour, and also because we stopped a couple of times for coffee, bread and pâté in the squares of delightful little villages.

The weather changed towards evening. When we reached the campsite the sky was leaden with cloud, and rain was lashing down. We'd arrived just in time: there were only a few places left on which to pitch a tent.

With the help of the boys, I put up the huge compartment tent I'd bought from my friend John Bowler, consultant physician at Winchcombe Hospital, thankful for the rehearsals we'd had on the lawn at home. C. P. and Joyce were going to sleep in a tiny two-man tent he had borrowed from a cartoonist friend of his. If the cartoonist was in search of material, he certainly got plenty from the stories when we got back.

The two-man tent had one basic drawback: it didn't have a flysheet.

So wherever C. P. or Joyce touched the canvas – and it was impossible not to in the confined space – water would start seeping in. The contortions they went through trying to avoid the drips would have earned them a diploma in advanced yoga.

Finally, they settled down in their sleeping bags. Just as Joyce was nodding off she woke up with a start and said, 'Christopher John!' – she used C. P.'s full title when she was annoyed –'Christopher John! Stop that!'

'Stop what?' murmured C. P. sleepily.

'You know very well what,' said Joyce. 'We're having none of that in this little tent!'

'I never touched you,' said C. P. Or at least he started to say it when he, too, felt a nudge from under the groundsheet.

He put his ear close to the spot and heard a muffled 'Eek-eek . . .'

Rats!

As he found out next day, he'd pitched the tent in the gathering dusk over a series of rat holes, and now the occupants were trying to get out for their night's scavenging.

'Er . . . yes, Pet. Sorry about that,' he said, sitting up in his sleeping bag and batting hard at the groundsheet as if he were trying to get comfortable. Thankfully, it worked. The rats

were either scared off by C. P.'s clouting or found another exit.

Joyce had had a phobia about rats ever since seeing a TV version of *1984*, and no tent in the world would have contained her had she suspected there was a family of them under the groundsheet. But suspecting nothing worse than that C. P. had been getting frisky in a confined space and inappropriate circumstances, she drifted off happily to sleep.

Next day C. P. dismantled the tent and lifted the ground-sheet to reveal several well-used rat holes. The scream Joyce let out was some indication of what her reaction would have been the night before: she jumped into the van, slammed the door, and refused to come out until the tent had been re-pitched on a rat-free piece of ground and the offending holes filled in.

We were staying a couple of days at this campsite, the idea being that we would get acclimatised to France. With the cold and damp weather, we became more acclimatised to a wet weekend in Llandudno. Still, we had fun.

Paul and Clive, who were then only in their teens, went down to the local bar and sampled their first French beer, feeling very adult and devilish. It's difficult to believe that both are married now, with a child each, and that Clive is teaching in Germany.

Jane was a couple of years younger than Janet, and thought it marvellous to have this 16-year-old sophisticate as a friend. They talked and giggled far into the night, discussing pop stars and teeny-bopper heart throbs whose names I'd never even heard. Again, its hard to believe that Jane is now 23, a dress designer and theatre stage door-keeper and that Janet is a Fleet Street journalist.

We all ate in the main tent. As we started on the coffee after breakfast, peering out at the sheeting rain and trying hard not to shiver, C. P. had a brilliant idea.

'It's a bit early in the day, Bob,' he said, producing a bottle of duty-free brandy, 'but I think a drop of this in the coffee will work wonders for our chests.'

It did, too. Before very long, the weather didn't seem so bad after all.

The rain kept up. Brandy in the coffee became a regular mealtime treat and, if the truth were to be told, something to be taken as an anti-damp specific between meals.

The next leg of our journey looked, on paper, like a straight run, but it turned out to be up and down, round and about, and a real grind. We had managed to find room in the van for a case of French wine. C. P. promoted himself to wine manager and happily nursed the case in the back, sampling it now and again to make sure that it was travelling reasonably well.

Eventually we arrived at a most beautiful campsite at Argentat, dominated by a large château, and with pine forests surrounding a great lake.

The château offered some social amenities, including a *plat du jour*: sometimes steak or fish with chips. It saved our girls cooking, and the chips made C. P. feel more at home.

For the first couple of days the rain still came down, and we kept up with C. P.'s prescription for our chests. By the time the sun came out on the third morning, we'd drunk all our duty-free except for a bottle of bacardi rum.

'Amazing,' said C. P. 'But at least we won't have all that extra weight to carry around.'

The bacardi had its own medicinal uses. With the sun came swarms of gnats, all of which seemed to home in on my bald spot. Within minutes I was covered in angry bites.

'Here,' said C. P., brandishing the bacardi. 'Rub some of this on. It'll keep them away and take some of the sting out.'

'Are you sure?'

'Positive,' he said. 'Never been known to fail.'

The Frenchman in the tent opposite looked in amazement at the mad English: one sitting on a folding stool, the other dabbing him on the head with what he could have sworn was bacardi rum.

(It worked, though. Whether or not it was my trust in C. P.'s faith in the curative powers of bacardi, I don't know. But the stings eased a bit and the gnats seemed to keep away after that.)

The Frenchman opposite certainly got his money's worth. He'd heard that the English were eccentric, but this was something else. He was fascinated by the goings-on and spent most of his day watching us. He even arranged his table outside his tent so that he wouldn't miss anything at mealtimes.

C. P. decided to take the lads fishing. He wrote the *Tadchester Gazette*'s angling column, and a session at the lake by the château promised some nice copy.

'What about bait?' I asked.

'No problem,' said C. P. 'We've got some cheese, and we can rescue some of that stale bread.'

The eight of us consumed vast quantities of French bread, which is only palatable when it's fresh. Any bread left at the end of the day was consigned to the camp dustbins.

C. P. went down to the dustbins and returned with armfuls of old bread. The Frenchman watched in horror. Not only were the English mad, they were incredibly hard up, raiding the dustbins for their daily bread. He missed his mouth with the croissant he was eating, and collected a noseful of crumbs.

C. P. and the lads did quite well on the lake, returning the fish alive from their keepnets to the water, as befitted humane British anglers. The French took away everything they caught, down to the tiniest tiddler, to make into bouillabaise.

'Bloody barbarians,' muttered C. P.

The next morning, Clive and Paul were stricken with the gripes, a result of overdoing the food and drink in the local bistro the night before. After rushing to the latrines and violently throwing up, they both stretched out on the ground outside their tent, pale and sweating, and groaning loudly.

The Frenchman watched, horrified. Serve *les Anglais* right for eating all that stale bread. This time his ruminations were interrupted by his fork, which missed his mouth and jabbed him painfully in the ear.

When the lads recovered, we packed up for the next stage of our journey and moved off, leaving behind us a very disappointed Frenchman. No more mealtime cabarets from the English eccentrics.

We were all excited about the villa. 'You'll enjoy it,' I said. 'For what we're paying, it must be good. These villas are really superb: marble bathrooms, huge iron cooking ranges, old oak beams, scrubbed pine tables. The French really know how to look after these old places.'

What I had forgotten was that we were hiring this place from an Englishman, and an English doctor to boot.

We had a pleasant, meandering drive through the most beautiful countryside, with C. P. in the back overseeing the wine, and eventually reached the farm that had been given as a landmark.

The only other building in the vicinity was a broken-down barn-like building with its shutters up. We were standing outside the barn, consulting the map, when a buxom middle-aged lady approached us from the farm. In halting French, I asked her the whereabouts of the villa.

'*Ici*,' she said, pointing at the barn.

'*Ici*?' I cried. 'You mean *this*?'

'*Oui, Monsieur*,' she said, beaming proudly. And then, looking serious, she asked if there were any young children in the party.

'Nobody under the age of 14,' I said.

'Good,' she said. 'Because I have just put the rat poison down.'

My God! This ruin was our villa – and it was infested with rats!

At this point Joyce nearly fainted. Rats under the tent were bad enough. But rats in our luxury villa . . .

I turned the huge key presented to me by the farmer's wife and pushed open the creaking door. Inside, we were greeted by the spectacle of naked light bulbs hanging on cords from cracked and peeling ceilings. For eight of us there were only six chairs. The kitchen contained a few rusting and rudimentary cooking appliances and a large rickety table. The upper rooms contained beds whose mattresses appeared to be stuffed with rejects from the local brickyard. In a corner of every room was a pile of poisoned bran.

There was a visitors' book in the hallway, scribbled over with strange messages. One said, 'Be kind to our four-legged friends,' and another read, 'Man the lifeboat when it rains.' Our four-legged friends we were to meet soon enough. When it rained towards the end of the week we were wishing we did have a lifeboat: the roof had more than a few tiles missing. I realised that I must have had a few tiles missing myself, to have booked the place at all. Luxurious, it was not.

However, we soon made the best of it. We had sunshine, we had a balcony, we had grapes we could pick off the verandah. In the village beyond the farm was a little shop which sold very drinkable wine at a few francs a bottle. Before we had even unpacked, C. P. and the lads had slipped up the road and returned lugging a couple of crates between them: the shop-keeper's entire stock.

'Look at this!' chortled C. P. 'Cheap enough to wash the floor with! And there's even money back on the bottles.'

Things got off to a rousing start that night with a firework festival in the village. A squad of drum majorettes arrived, dressed in bright uniforms with cowboy boots and very skimpy skirts: a spectacle that did not go unappreciated by the lads nor, I must confess, by C. P. and myself.

Then the village band turned up to lead them. Or it would have led them if the bandleader had not popped into the bistro for a quick one. The quick one became two quick ones, then three or four slower ones. Outside, the bronzed thighs of the drum majorettes were turning blue and goose-pimply in the cool evening air.

Every so often one of the bandsmen would rush in and indicate that the bandleader's presence was respectfully but urgently requested. But with the French equivalent of 'Just one for the road, old boy,' he would order up another drink.

Finally, in came a bugler, whose entreaties, like the others', were ignored. In desperation, he put his bugle to his lips and at point-blank range blew a blast of the 'Marseillaise' into the bandleader's left ear. The maestro took the hint and staggered out, wincing and clutching his ear, to lead the parade.

They made a fine sight, with the band and the drum majorettes keeping perfect step, even if the bandleader didn't. The girls goose-pimples soon disappeared, and a good time was had by all.

It was a lively, noisy, tuneful and enjoyable evening, with a performance out of all proportion to the size of the tiny village. Clive and Paul practised their A-Level French by chatting up

some of the local girls. Any further hopes of a spot of *entente cordiale* were dashed by the presence in the shadows of several large French *mamans*. Marshal Pétain's resolve at Verdun – 'They shall not pass!' – had nothing on that of the average French matron.

'Never mind,' said Paul to Clive. 'They'd all grow up like their mothers anyway. We'd soon be fighting out of our weight.'

Back at the villa, which in the light of the naked bulbs made the House of Usher look like an Ideal Homes showplace, we enjoyed a leisurely supper. Ominous scuttling sounds from darkened corners, and from the rafters above the table, indicated that our four-legged friends were willing to clear up any leftovers.

'I want to go to the toilet,' said Joyce, 'but I'm scared stiff.'

'Leave it to me,' said Clive. He picked up a tin tray and marched into the bathroom banging it loudly. 'Nothing in there, Mum,' he said. 'You'll be perfectly safe.'

Joyce went in the bathroom and closed the door. All was quiet for a couple of minutes, and then came a piercing shriek of, 'Rats! Let me out!'

Poor Joyce had been washing her hands when from behind a piece of broken panelling had padded a huge rat, which must have mistaken the tin tray for a dinner gong. Her screams sent it scuttling back again, but it wasn't the best preparation for a good night's sleep.

Fishing in the area was good, and we bought licences at the local bicycle shop. C. P. had some trouble asking for a tin of maggots, until he discovered that the French name for them was *asticots*. He was horrified to discover that the container was little bigger than a tobacco tin and that it held only a few dozen scrawny bluebottle maggots.

'God!' he exclaimed. 'In Britain we'd get ten times that amount for half the price!'

But he wasn't in Britain, and that was the best the shop could offer. Grudgingly, he pocketed the tin and set off for the river.

He didn't do too well on that trip, reeling in just a few small roach. It seemed that even the fish weren't too keen on the

24

locally-bred *asticots*. And what made it worse was the Great Maggot Explosion.

Keeping his eye on the float, he pulled out a tin from his pocket and filled his pipe. Still keeping an eye on the float, he struck a match, applied it to the bowl of the pipe, and inhaled deeply.

There was a series of sharp explosions and an ammoniac smell as if an old stable was burning down. C. P. broke into a massive coughing fit, dropped his rod, and staggered around with watering eyes.

'Bloody Norah!' he gasped, and pulled the tin from his pocket.

It wasn't his tobacco tin at all, but the tin of *asticots*. The explosions had been half a dozen unfortunate maggots and the ammoniac smell was the smoke from the sawdust they were packed in.

'How was it?' I asked, when his coughing had subsided, trying hard not to laugh, but soon giving up.

'I can't recommend it,' he wheezed. 'It'll never replace the old-fashioned Three Nuns.'

The eight of us explored some of the towns nearby, enjoying a cup of coffee, glass of beer or a cognac at the boulevard cafes, soaking up the atmosphere and generally watching the world go by.

C. P. even developed a taste for French beer and would squeeze in an extra swift one when it was time to go home. 'Home' was still the villa, where the rats had become bolder and would appear on top of the cooking range or the huge kitchen dresser. After the wives and children had gone to bed, C. P. and I used to sit up on rat-watching duties with a glass of wine in one hand and a heavy walking boot in the other. When a rat appeared we would let fly with a boot.

Whether it was the wine, the unwieldy missiles, or that we were just not good at boot-throwing, our aim was not up to Bisley standards. By the end of the week we'd not hit a single rat, but had severely depleted the villa's small collection of crockery.

On our last day it rained heavily. Water poured through the roof and down the walls. The lifeboat would have come in very handy. Still, we'd had fun.

'Tell me again,' I said to C. P. as we mopped the sodden floors. 'We *have* had fun, haven't we?'

After a tiring two-day haul back to the Channel coast, we stayed overnight in Calais at a very comfortable hotel. The bill for our rooms, a few litres of wine and a very liberal *petit déjeuner* came to about half what the English equivalent would cost. It was just as well, because by now we were flat broke, with not even enough cash to stock up again at the duty-free shop.

The hovercraft crossing was rough – there had been some debate as to whether the sea was too rough to risk the crossing – and several of the passengers were violently sick. A bunch of them at the back blamed their sickness on the smoke from the pipes which C. P. and I were puffing at contentedly. Our children, who overheard them discussing the practicalities of a maritime lynching party, pretended not to be with us.

'Don't know when they're well off,' said C. P. as we put out our pipes in deference to the cries and threats from behind. 'I could have been smoking those bloody maggots again.'

So that was France: sunshine, rain, food poisoning, exploding maggots, the House of Usher and all. Our wives and children voted it the best holiday they'd ever had.

Even C. P. said he'd known worse.

CHAPTER 4

Family Matters

Most people say, when their children leave home, how much easier life is.

I've not found this to be true. After the children's schooling, there's university or polytechnic. After that there's marriage. After that there are houses and after that there are grandchildren. Instead of parental worries decreasing as our children get older, they seem to increase.

Our elder son Trevor, after taking a couple of law degrees, decided that it was an actor's life for him and became a successful actor-writer.

It was great fun to follow him around seeing his stage performances. Of his more recent shows, *Caught in the Act* was the funniest farce I've ever seen. It was at the Royal Exchange Theatre, Manchester, and starred Michael Denison and Gabrielle Drake of *Crossroads* TV fame. Hopefully it was going to go to the West End.

Trevor always seemed to be in work. He followed the performance at Manchester by having a large if not major part in a TV series called *Star Cops*. This is not going to make him an overnight star but should make him a familiar face on television. He did achieve transient fame in a Shell TV commercial, where he was jumping about behind a counter. Then he was flown to Germany for a day to do a liqueur advertisement. Because of his TV commitments, he was unable to do a day's filming in New Zealand which would have meant his spending a week there.

He had in the previous year become the New Zealand Schweppes man. This meant a week's filming as several characters which included a yokel, a butler and a barmaid – possibly the biggest barmaid in the world.

Some months after this advert had been shown in New Zealand, he heard that not only had he received the Gold Award presented by their commercial television for the best character in television adverts, but also the Silver and Bronze.

The awards are in the form of medals which he wears on his dinner jacket at formal dinners, just to confuse everybody.

Although they lived a long way away, our children were still able to present me with various medical problems and alarms.

On one of my rare trips to London, when lunching at the Lansdowne Club with the film and theatre director, Peter Cotes, I was paged on the telephone. It was my younger son Paul, ringing from a hotel at London Airport where his electronic components firm was holding an exhibition.

He said that he'd started to vomit some black stuff, and now was vomiting blood. What should he do?

I told him to get himself driven to Reading Hospital to the Casualty Department, where I knew one of the surgeons. I abandoned my lunch and caught the first train to Reading.

Happily nothing was seriously amiss, although they did have to take him to theatre and poke a tube down him to make sure.

As most of Paul's work lay in the west of England, his firm asked him to move further west. He and his wife Gill were living in a tiny cottage in Aldermaston, a lovely old Jacobean village spoilt by the traffic. His cottage was further spoilt by the fact that most of the traffic seemed to enter the front bedroom at five o'clock in the morning, and leave via the bathroom.

They put their house up for sale. Their sale, as well as the usual ups and downs and near-sales, was further complicated by the fact that our dear daughter-in-law Gill had now become pregnant. Pam's great ambition of becoming a grandmother was about to be achieved.

Paul had nearly sold his house about six times when they eventually found a positive buyer, a very young lady whose only problem was that she was having some trouble with selling her own house. Not that she hadn't found a buyer, but her particular purchaser was extremely difficult. His first demand was that the sale could only go through if the purchase was completed on the 8 August. This was the day Gill's baby was due. It was so important that Paul didn't lose his sale that he had to agree.

Paul and Gill were buying a lovely little town house in Cirencester, Gloucestershire. The owners of the house, a Mr and Mrs Morgan, had taken Paul and Gill to their hearts. They had not only given them masses of furniture, but told them not to worry about dates. They'd already bought the house they were moving to and, whatever happened to anybody else, the Cirencester house was Paul's and Gill's. This was a great weight off their minds.

Liz, Gill's mother, had come back from India: not only was Gill having a baby, but her elder sister Joanna was also expecting four weeks before Gill's baby was due.

The months seemed to fly by, and I kept in constant touch. One evening I rang the house to see how Gill was. Liz answered the phone and said, 'Oh, she's resting.'

What I didn't know was that she was resting in Basingstoke Hospital, and a few hours later Paul rang to say that we were grandparents to a dear little girl called Daisy May. Pam was over the moon.

Daisy May had arrived a fortnight early, well ahead of moving day, which was very thoughtful of her.

As well as being fortunate with the Morgans, Paul was also lucky with his solicitor, a Mr Kaxe of Gardner and Leader at Thatcham, who really put himself out on their behalf.

Just after the birth of the baby he had to break the news to Paul that the man who was buying Paul's purchaser's house, and who had insisted that they move on the 8 August, now said he couldn't move until the 28th. They had no alternative but to fit in with this request.

Mr Kaxe came into his own when the second moving date was looming. Suddenly the solicitor of the man who was buying the house from Paul's purchaser presented the young girl with 100 points to answer. She managed to answer 99 but he refused to accept anybody's word about the hundredth: he wanted it in writing.

When the girl said that she would send it round by car – and this meant a journey of 60 or 70 miles – he confessed what the real trouble was: the man wasn't ready for the move and everything would have to be postponed for a further week.

It created a problem; the exchange of contracts was only a few days before the completion date, the said 28th. This delaying tactic meant there was no possibility of their completing on that date, the day Paul actually planned to move and for which, for the second time, he had the furniture vans organised.

On the 27th, the difficult solicitor promised Mr Kaxe that he would exchange contracts on the 28th. Mr Kaxe asked if I could bridge Paul for a week. If so, his move could go ahead on the 28th, providing contracts were exchanged on that day, and the removal vans wouldn't have to be cancelled.

I scraped my coffers bare and just managed to produce the right amount.

The day of the move dawned but there was more trouble in store. First, Paul's furniture van broke down on the way to him. The next van that came wasn't big enough, so they had to send away for a trailer. They were almost completely packed, when Mr Kaxe said they might have to unpack again. He had that morning telephoned the difficult solicitor to formalise the exchange and found that the chap was not in the office – he had gone away and was in fact moving house himself.

31

Phones were buzzing all over the place. Meanwhile, there was Paul, sitting with his packed furniture outside his house.

Eventually Mr Kaxe managed to get hold of the senior partner of the chap who'd disappeared, so did the solicitor of the girl who was buying Paul's house, and the Morgans' solicitors from Cirencester joined in. Together the three solicitors threatened to approach the Law Society if something wasn't done.

The senior partner of the firm was quite unaware of what had been going on. He went down to his junior's office and found complete chaos. He managed to sort things out, and by lunchtime had exchanged contracts.

The go-ahead to Paul and Gill came through and the furniture went off. Gill, Liz and Daisy May arrived safely in Cirencester to find that the kindly Morgans had left them milk and bread as a welcome present.

So, happily, it all ended well. After I'd sweated for a week at the prospect of my life savings going down the drain, completion date did follow up as promised and my money was safely returned.

Moving to Cirencester meant that Paul and Gill were marginally nearer to us in Tadchester, but with Trevor and Jane sharing a flat in Brighton, we were rather strung out as a family.

I still talked about my offspring as our children, though Trevor now was more than 30, Paul was approaching it and even little Jane was 23.

Jane was busy trying to establish herself as a dress designer. She had this terrible logo, which looked like a pair of false teeth shouting DUFF, stuck on all the dresses and T-shirts she made.

Having been initially disappointed about some promised shop premises, she'd been going round markets to sell her dresses. Now a few friends, each with a special skill to offer, managed to obtain a tiny shop in part of Aladdin's Cave at Brighton.

One of the friends made jewellery, one bags, one hats, and two of them made dresses and shirts. I don't think any of them was making a profit, they were just about breaking even, but they'd made a start.

Jane kept the wolf from the door by being the night stage door-keeper at the Royal Theatre, Brighton. They had many pre-London runs in Brighton and it was interesting to hear how nice the vast majority of the really big stars were who took part.

Jane was often given a bunch of flowers, a box of chocolates, or some other gift for her help as stage door-keeper. She was always treated politely and generously.

We enjoyed visiting Trevor and Jane in Brighton. The only problem was that their flat was about five storeys up and I always felt I needed an oxygen mask by the time I'd reached the top.

The flat was a great boon for both Trevor and Jane. Trevor, who worked all over the place, particularly in London, was most often able to commute from Brighton. They both loved Brighton itself with its shops, cinemas, eating houses and pier. You could just see the sea from their lounge window and everything was so close at hand. With good local transport and a good train service to London, they hardly needed a car.

Life had changed for us in that instead of us looking forward to the children coming home, we now had to make the long journeys to Cirencester and Brighton to visit them in their homes.

Paul worked very hard and conscientiously at his job, which meant doing a lot of his bookwork on Sundays. Jane, with six nights at the theatre was very tied down, and when Trevor was on location he was hardly available at all. But it was a great comfort to see them all settling down, doing well, and working so hard.

We were very proud of them.

*   *   *

We had a bereavement in the family. Our little Cairn terrier, Suzie, who had been getting blinder and deafer, finally went to sleep one day and never woke up again.

She was 17 years old.

We had had her since she was nine months and she'd been an absolute joy. In the end we weren't sorry to see her go because she'd lost all appreciation of any real quality of life; she couldn't see properly, she couldn't hear properly, she bumped into the furniture, and she couldn't tell one member of the family from another. The only instinct she had left was for food, and she would eat anything that was put near her.

Happily, her end was peaceful and we buried her in a quiet little spot in the garden.

Suzie had a pedigree as long as your arm but her teeth were a bit crooked. Perhaps she'd been reared to breed or to show and was not good enough for either. But we fell for her as soon as we saw her.

We hadn't told the children we were buying a new dog, Pam had just said when she'd brought them home from school that there was a surprise. They opened the front door and there, on the top of the stairs, was this tiny dog. Instantly Suzie rolled over on her back, presenting a little hairy tummy to be scratched. Immediately she was one of the family.

She followed the children everywhere, and was part of every game. When there were no children about, she vigorously chased rabbits all over the garden.

Only once was she ever successful in her chase, catching a tiny baby rabbit which happily she didn't harm. We were able to disengage it from her mouth and it ran away back to its mother.

She was marvellous at Hunt the Chocolate Button; she knew all the rules of the game. She would be sent outside the room and the chocolate button would be hidden somewhere. To great excitement the door would be opened. Suzie would charge in, sniff all over the room, and never fail to find her prize.

Over the years she had some very amorous encounters, particularly with the little Pomeranian down the road, but she never actually had any puppies. She did have one or two false pregnancies which were terribly distressing to her. These didn't disappear until she had a hysterectomy.

She had become ill, drinking copious amounts of water, and we couldn't understand what was wrong.

The vet diagnosed precisely: a septic uterus. After her operation she soon changed from a sickly dog into a bright and happy one again.

We missed her sadly. Now with both dog and children gone, the house seemed to echo around us.

*   *   *

We decided to have another dog and Pam set her heart on a West Highland White terrier. There didn't seem to be too many about, but we eventually found in the local paper an advertisement for a bitch just the other side of Winchcombe. We rang and enquired about her and decided to call in on our way to visit Paul and Gill. If we liked the dog, we could pick her up on the way back.

We both knew perfectly well that we'd buy her as soon as we saw her. We arrived at a lovely old thatched cottage. Outside was an adult West Highland, tied to a stake. According to the owner (who led us to assume that the dog was the mother) she had to be kept tied up because she was so fond of water. Loose on her own she'd be straight down to the river, would be a long time away and very wet when she came back.

We were taken into the kitchen where a tiny quiet fluffy little dog, snow-white from a recent bath, was exploring the floor. She was a bit quiet, but lovely. We paid our money and agreed to pick her up in two days' time, at the end of our visit to Paul and Gill.

Before we set off on our way home from Paul's, we rang up to say what time we'd be calling. The daughter of the house said 'Hang on, I'll get mother.'

Mother came sobbing to the phone to say there'd been a terrible accident – the puppy had got out of the yard and the Land Rover had run over it.

They did have another puppy left from the litter but he was a male. Would we like to have a look at him?

We were terribly disappointed, especially Pam. We said we'd come and have a look at him but my suspicions were aroused a bit.

People who misused drugs, and were trying to get extra supplies, usually told one of three classical stories: One, that the drugs had fallen out on the drive and a car had run over them. Two, that the cabinet had fallen off the bathroom wall and the dog had eaten them. Three, the most common of all, that they'd left them in the pocket of their jeans and had put the jeans in the washing machine.

The story of the Land Rover sounded very much like one of these, but perhaps my years in medicine had give me a too-suspicious nature. We were buying a dog, for heaven's sake. I immediately put such unworthy thoughts from my mind.

When we got there we were completely charmed with the little puppy. He was much livelier than his little sister, recently deceased. Straightaway we named him Billy, and agreed to take him instead.

The lady of the house gave us a great bowl of prepared food, some sort of tripe concoction. She gave instructions to feed him only on this and to make certain that he went the next day to the vet to have his parvo injection.

We brought Billy home and he was absolutely gorgeous, running about on the grass and chasing the ball.

We took him to the vet's the next day. The vet thought he was a bit young for the injection, but in spite of this gave him the lot, parvo, hardpad and distemper.

Twenty-four hours after the injection, Billy started vomiting. We returned him to the vet, who said that this was quite normal when a puppy was settling into a new habitat.

He wasn't much better the next day so I rang up, to be told by a rather snooty receptionist, 'Stop worrying. This is how puppies always are.' I accepted that I only knew about human ailments and that perhaps she was right, but I certainly would have been worried if he'd been a human being.

Billy got worse and I spent the whole of the night with the little chap, who was obviously very poorly in my arms.

We took him to the vet again the next day, who now agreed that he was very poorly, and that he had only a 50-50 chance of survival. Billy was admitted to their little animal hospital, where he died 24 hours later.

It was amazing how upsetting was the loss of this little puppy that we'd had only five days. We were heartbroken.

Samples had to be sent off to find the cause of his death. They took some time to come back but we eventually found that he had died of parvo virus. The fact that he'd been given an injection while he had it would certainly have diminished his chances of survival. This particular virus meant that we couldn't have any dog to visit the house for six months, and if we did decide to have a new dog in six months' time, he would have to have been immunised against parvo before he came.

I got in touch with the lady we'd bought the dog from, and broke the news. She was horrified, but on closer questioning revealed that the lovely old adult dog outside wasn't his mother; that he had in fact come from Wales, from a friend down there. I was offered my money back but, being soft, only accepted half. I didn't pursue the matter, but I had my suspicions that Billy and his sister might have come from the kind of mercenary and heartless puppy farms we read about now and again. Nor did I entirely believe that the sister had been run over: she might have met the same fate as Billy.

So for six months we were dogless – not even friends could bring dogs round to see us – but we were determined not to make the same mistake again.

A patient of mine, Mrs Gater, who ran the Spire Ridge Kennels, said she would get a puppy from a breeder for us and keep it until after it had had its first injection.

That's how we obtained our Bertie. He wasn't an instant replacement for Suzie, who'd been with us for so long, but was as lovable a little dog as you could find anywhere.

He was terribly good natured. You could take a bone from his mouth, he was as soft as butter. There were only two things he really disliked. One was wheels: for some reason he would dash at anything on wheels. The other was papers or letters being delivered through the letter box. If we weren't about he'd try and pick them out of the letter box himself, and he'd rush about, up and down the stairs, until the paperboy or the postman had gone. But he loved all people and all dogs. Each day, Pam would take him for walks along the river bank, where he'd meet all sorts of friends.

We spoiled him, I'm afraid. He jumped on chairs, used to climb up the side of my armchair, sit on the back, and try and lick my nose.

When Pam was away, visiting Paul and Gill and grand-daughter, Bertie would climb up on the back of my chair and sleep precariously on the top, just touching my head to make sure I was still there.

When I walked him along the river bank, I found I had no ordinary dog – everybody knew him. I've always been a bit frightened of big dogs and when I saw some great Afghan hound or an Alsatian bounding towards us, I'd slip the lead on, only to hear the owner shout, 'Oh, that's Bertie! It's all right – they're friends!' And Bertie would go off cavorting in the long grass. He was a real pleasure and the house rang to his barks.

He was a great watchdog, standing for ages looking out of the lounge window, one paw on the sill. As Paul said, he'd bark at a falling leaf. Gill said perhaps he was born in Barkshire!

There was one aspect about him that worried me. He made me think, for the first time, that reincarnation is possible. He was a sort of cross between a prostitute and a missionary.

If he could get into the bedroom he would run in, jump up and lie on the pillow, legs astride, with an expression that said, 'Come and get me.' There was something voluptuous about it.

He was never allowed in the bedroom at night and, in fact, was a very good dog at bedtime. On command, he would go off to his basket in the kitchen and never, even from his first night, cause a fuss.

The missionary side of him appeared when he watched television. He was the only dog I'd met that was a television addict.

During Wimbledon fortnight you'd see his head go from side to side, following the ball. But if either sex or violence appeared on the screen he went absolutely mad, jumping up, scratching at the screen and trying to interfere.

Jane called him Bertie Whitehouse and said he ought to go on the Watch Dog Committee – he would have made an ideal censor. In fact his taste was quite discriminating. He loved nature programmes and would watch quite happily and then go round to the back of the television set to see where the animals had gone to.

Although, at times, Bertie did make me wonder what he'd been in a previous life one reassuring fact which made me feel that he was a dog, and only a dog, was that he had a girlfriend, an 11-year-old Jack Russell bitch called Lilly. They could sense each other as if by radar; if Bertie's tail wagged in a certain way we knew Lilly was round the corner. With tails wagging like propellers they tore up and down the river bank chasing each other and playing with enormous exuberance. They were a joy to watch. Occasionally they would stop and play something completely different. Then there was no doubt that Bertie was a dog.

CHAPTER 5

Just Deserts

One of the great joys of taking the children on holiday was their bubbling excitement when we were taking them somewhere new, particularly if we were renting a cottage or an apartment.

Among the first cottages we ever rented was Mermaid Cottage in Virgin Street, St. Ives, Cornwall. We liked it so much that eventually we went there two or three times. The children loved it because it was quite close to the harbour and beach, quite close to the town and far too close to the amusement arcade, where they would nip off and spend all their pennies given half a chance.

It had a stable door. You opened the top half of the door, stood behind it and watched the world and his wife go by. With a view from a stable door, even washing-up could be made interesting.

We often visited Wales at Easter. There was always great excitement when we arrived at a new cottage: all the rooms had to be explored, decisions to be made as to who slept where. But there'd be hardly any sleep that night because there were fresh discoveries to be made in the morning. Where were the nearest shops? Where was the nearest beach? There were a hundred and one things to find out.

We had a flat in Solva, Dyfed, overlooking a beautiful tree-lined creek which wound down to the sea.

We had a farmhouse in Haverford West with a trout stream, or a supposed trout stream, running through the four acres of ground that went with it. We never caught anything in the stream but we could always, as most fishermen do, live in hope.

We had a cottage near Milford Haven for the first holiday that Gill came on with us at the beginning of her eight-year courtship with Paul. On the way back home we stopped at a pub for lunch. After the meal, on the table in front of Paul was left a dirty plate, piled with odd bits of fish and chips and pie.

Paul's reaction was quite simple. He picked it up and handed it to Gill. Gill took the plate uncomplainingly and took it back to the bar.

I let Paul have a mouthful in the left ear for his discourtesy, but it was then I realised that one day they would probably get married.

*　　*　　*

We had several pleasant holidays in the Channel Islands. A short one in Guernsey which we loved, then a much longer one there after Trevor had fallen in Sark, broken his hip and been shipped to Guernsey. We had to attend him daily at the marvellous Princess Elizabeth Hospital.

Years earlier, Pam and I had gone with our friends Janice and Kevin Bird to Jersey. We'd been on holiday with them several times and this was probably the least successful, partly because the food at the hotel was so poor. The evening meal consisted of a miniscule portion of meat, one potato, one sprout and a couple of beans each. Afterwards we had to retire to the Chinese restaurant next door to supplement our diet.

Pam had just lost her mother. Jane, who was only a few months old and had been weaned hurriedly to give Pam a break, was left in the capable arms of her godmother, Zara, back in Tadchester.

42

We went round seeing the various sights, but the weather was indifferent so one evening we thought we'd go to the pictures. Pam had been silently worrying all the time about having left Jane at home. The title of the film was little comfort. In huge letters across the front of the cinema it demanded: *WHATEVER HAPPENED TO BABY JANE?* Kevin and Janice went in, but Pam couldn't face it. We went off and had a cream tea instead.

I once paid a visit to Jersey on my own. It was the beginning of my sabbatical leave: 13 whole weeks off. I was hoping to write most of a book in this break and wanted symbolically to break the pattern of work.

It was March. I couldn't get any sunshine locally, so I thought Jersey would be a change. I could work in peace and quiet, with just a chance of better weather. I booked in at one of the best hotels, which was inexpensive out of season.

What they'd forgotten to tell me was that they were completely renovating the hotel. When I arrived there, the corridors were filled with workmen. There was scaffolding all over the place and power saws going every day, augmented by the noise of riveting and banging. I had to disturb about five men every time I went in and out of my room. It rained all the time outside, and everything was shut down.

Eventually I came home early for some peace and quiet. In view of the circumstances, the tour operators refunded me some of my money.

*   *   *

It seemed that every time I went on holiday without Pam or the family, some sort of major disaster took place. Although I had a great number of experiences away from the family, I could hardly call them holidays.

There were two exceptions: my trans-Saharan crossings.

In *The Sunday Times* one day I saw advertised a trip across the Sahara, organised by an enterprising little travel firm. My patient partners agreed that I could disappear for five weeks in

43

the middle of winter on condition that I provided, and paid for, a locum.

I booked to fly out from London to Paris, to Toulon, to Algiers, to the Oasis of El Golea, then a 4,000-mile trip around the Sahara by Land Rover.

In Tadchester it was exciting news for the local gossips. The fact that I was leaving my wife for so long could only mean that we were breaking up.

As the time drew nearer, Pam's face was getting longer and longer. But on the strength of the fact that I was having an expensive trip she managed to get an expensive sewing machine out of me, explaining how much money she was going to save by making all her clothes while I was away.

The day finally came and I suddenly found myself at London Airport in a bush jacket, having hardly flown before, wondering what on earth I was doing. I was travelling with five other people who were booked on the same Saharan trip: a lady gynaecologist, a Yorkshire plumber, a vicar, an army officer who was spending his leave from Aden crossing the Sahara, and an artist who had some personal problem he wanted to get out of his system.

I was very apprehensive about flying. Just the bang as the plane took its wheels up made me think it was the end. This intrepid explorer had to be reassured by the passenger next to him.

A rather suspicious looking chap with a day's growth of beard hovered near us when we changed planes in Paris. He came up and introduced himself as an American anaesthetist. We found, reminiscing about our medical student days (he had trained in England), that we'd actually fought on the same programme when the hospital had boxed against Cambridge University. Halfway through the trip I asked why he hadn't made himself known to us in London.

'Now I can tell you,' he said. 'I'm Jewish. Travelling round Arab countries did not seem the most sensible thing to do. I only made up my mind I was definitely going when I reached Paris.'

We spent our first night in Algiers in the Hotel St. George,

44

where General Eisenhower had his wartime headquarters, then we flew on to the oasis of El Golea where the Land Rovers were based. There we met the leader of the party, an ex-Colonel from the Sudan Defence Force, a delightful chap called Tommy.

Thus began five magic weeks.

First we explored El Golea, a large administrative oasis of 15,000 inhabitants with its magnificent ruined fort Ksur, a reminder of the days when the Tuareg nomads were masters of the desert. The local hotel boasted that it had 30 lavatories; unfortunately nobody seemed to have cleaned them out for several years.

We eventually set off from El Golea, spending the first night at Fort Mirabelle, a disused French Foreign Legion fort. The bleak outlook of the mud fort, set in a barren and featureless plain, took away any thoughts of the Foreign Legion's being glamorous and gave some example of the stark brutality of the legionnaires' lives.

From Fort Mirabelle to the next oasis – In Salah – we crossed the Tademait Plateau. The plateau is similar to a bleak 500-mile aerodrome runway, as wide as it's long with a perpetual wind blowing. It's baking hot with scorching sunshine in the day, but freezing at night.

In Salah was, until the turn of the century, the base for the warlike Tuaregs and a crossroads for camel caravans and traders. It was also a slave market; it's only a few years since slaves were sold there and you can still find the odd slave pottering about. There was a constant battle with the sand which gradually seemed to be taking over the town. Leaving In Salah, we entered the Arak Gorge where there was some vegetation, game, gazelle and mountain sheep.

Travelling so far meant a good deal of sitting in a bumpy Land Rover, but setting up camp at the end of the day provided plenty of work for everyone. There was fuel to be fetched, fires to be lit, Land Rovers serviced, tents erected – all this apart from the routine cooking and washing up. The day usually finished with a drop of duty-free around the camp-fire. We stopped putting up tents after a couple of nights, sleeping out in the open under the clear desert sky, which made the stars appear so much nearer.

From the Arak Gorge the countryside became more broken and interesting. We travelled the great Hoggar route to reach Tamanrasset, a beautiful oasis 5,400 feet up, only developed during the last 70 years. It's clean, with tree-lined streets and looks fresh and in good order, with two hotels, several cafes, and even a cinema trying to establish itself.

We thought we'd try a meal out and visited the Cafe of Peace. We asked for a typical Algerian dish and were served egg and chips on enamel plates. The waiter managed to hold two plates and pick his nose at the same time. A clever trick, but we weren't impressed.

The Hoggar is composed of vast granite masses, partly covered with lava, which time has eroded into fantastic lunar shapes. After a few days in Tamanrasset, which included a trip up into Hoggar Mountain, we went to the hermitage of the French priest, Charles Foucald. Father Foucald set up the order of The Little Brothers and Sisters of Jesus, some of whom were in retreat at this spartan hermitage.

The members of this order impressed me more than any other group of people I have met. They don't preach, they don't teach, they just settle in deprived communities and live by example. They don't offer western medicine or any other special technical help.

One aristocratic French lady had been living under a tent with the Tuareg for 15 years, and one other little sister had been working in a South African factory and living amongst the poor. These two ladies had such an aura about them that I would genuinely not have been surprised to see haloes round their heads.

We then set off south for Agades in Niger, passing through some of the most beautiful scenery in the whole of the Sahara, stretches of golden sand broken from time to time by curiously shaped outcrops of rocks which looked like giant sculptures.

From Tamanrasset south there's less traffic and we navigated mainly by looking for the wheelmarks of the giant Saharan lorries that used the route. We crossed the Algeria-Niger border at a place called In Geuzzam, quite a frightening experience. It's rumoured that guerrilla fighters are trained there, and the border guards put every obstacle they could think of in our way and generally made things as difficult as possible for us.

Inside Niger was quite different, there was a sort of freedom about it. In northern Niger there's some vegetation and further south an almost East African type of scrubland. The area is frequented by nomads with their flocks of sheep, goats, cattle and camels. Game was plentiful; gazelle and ostrich would race away in the distance as we drove by.

Agades is one of the main crossroads of the Sahara, with a bustling market centre where camel caravans unload cargoes of salt and dates. It was an incredible sight at night to go into the market place where there were probably two or three thousand camels, hundreds of little fires, traders, silversmiths, blacksmiths and cooks. It was a scene straight from the Arabian Nights, spread out over half a mile.

We made a trip from Agades into the Air mountains which

revealed a completely different landscape; some of the foothills are inhabited by an almost negroid ethnic type living in beehive huts, a complete contrast to the nomad Tuaregs in their tents.

We went on to an area of tin mines; not mines as we think of them – the tin is taken from the surface. The village we visited had had some sort of missionary teachers who had taught the children to read and write, and some of the villagers could speak good French.

Having given them a taste for what lay in the outside world, the missionaries had left them in these primitive surroundings. It brought it home very much to me how important it is not to interfere with a settled way of life: the teaching and do-gooding had broken up a community and made the young people dissatisfied with their life at home. Their only alternative was to hang around the towns in the oases 500 or 600 miles away or try and get casual work at the oil wells that were beginning to spring up.

One excitement in the village was when we were called to help a man who had fallen 40 feet down into the communal well. With ropes from the Land Rover we managed to haul him out, to the cheers of the surrounding villagers. There were more cheers when I offered him five francs to do it again.

We had a real adventure crossing the Tenere desert. It's not many years since this was first negotiated by a motor vehicle. Called the Dreaded Tenere Desert, it consists of 500 miles of

flat sand between Agades in Niger and Bilma, which is the sort of Siberia of Niger. As well as being an important salt-producing area, it is also a penal settlement.

The desert is swept by sandstorms on an average of one every two or three days and no one is allowed to cross without one of the few guides who know its routes and dangers. It's a 500-mile stretch with only one waterhole marked by a single tree, 'the only tree in the Tenere Desert'. This tree is unique in that it's the only tree to feature on maps of the world.

The Tenere is magnificent; miles of flat sand like an eternal beach. There are two routes: the easy one to the north which is uninterrupted flat sand and the more difficult route to the south, which we took on my second trip when we crossed with guides through the sand sea to explore the rarely visited oasis of Fachi with its medieval fort structure.

On reaching the Bilma Oasis with its salt mines and gardens, we paused for a rest and a couple of camel rides, then headed north through broken country, back into Algeria, to an oasis called Djanet at the foot of the Tassili Plateau.

I have climbed and spent a few days on the Plateau twice, and it's similar to my visual image of Conan Doyle's Lost World. We climbed up from the lush oasis of Djanet through barren rocky strata to come out at 6,000 feet on to this fascinating and ever-changing landscape of trees and water and fantastic rock shapes carved out by the gales.

One of the main objects of the expedition was to study the profusion of prehistoric carvings in the area; frescoes first discovered in the Twenties by a Frenchman called Henri Lhote. Some of the frescoes are not cave paintings, but drawings cut in the overhanging ledges in the warren-like canyons of the plateau and spread over a large area. Concentrations of the best are found near the approaches of the plateau and include figures of elephants, giraffes, hippopotami and rhinoceroses, which disappeared from this area thousands of years ago.

Then came the journey back via Djanet with a different view of Algeria, mushrooming oil wells and the oases of Ouargla and Hassi Messaoued with some sophisticated shops. Then there was the transport centre of In Amenas which seemed to be filled with Poles, Czechs or Russians – but with not a woman in the place. It could easily have been a Wild West town except there were no cowboy hats – there was something quite frightening about it.

We had our last stop near El Golea and then came the real tragedy of our present times – the speed of travel. On both Sahara trips I went on, after our first or second day we discarded our tents and slept in sleeping bags out on the sand. I'd lived in the open for five weeks, away from what we would call civilisation, with a small group of people. After I'd slept in the desert the night before and had breakfast in El Golea, it was frightening that I was home for tea in Tadchester that afternoon.

Still, I came back with the best suntan I've ever had, and with a great love for deserts.

I did some medical work for this adventurous little travel company and was invited a couple of years later to repeat the trip, taking round some rich Americans and acting as medical officer. Even going on almost the same route a second time did nothing to dispel the magic of the journey.

We were led this time by Ken, a young bearded Scotsman, and Julie, a superb cook, both experienced desert travellers, and Jim, the engineer of the party. We weren't exactly roughing it in the desert: our first meal out after El Golea consisted of soup, game pie filling with tinned new potatoes, peas and a bottle of Algerian red wine, followed by canned fruit, condensed milk, cheese, coffee and a bottle of white wine. By the time we had reached Djanet before our climb to see the Tassili frescos, Ken and Julie had fallen in love. Jim wanted to work on the Land Rover engines so the three of them decided to stay in Djanet and let me take the party up to the plateau. As none of our Americans spoke any French, my French was the only link between our guides and donkey drivers.

On the way up we bumped into a couple of Swiss, a journalist, Bernard Joliat, and his friend, a motorcyclist named Dede. They were hopelessly ill-equipped for such a venture, their main equipment being cameras, and their footwear only gym shoes.

All my boy-scouting instincts came to the fore as I proudly led my team of eight Americans, one Englishman, two Swiss, two guides, three donkey boys and eleven donkeys. I got them all up and back safely and Bernard and his wife, who visited us in England later, have remained friends of mine ever since.

Not only had the tour of the plateau done me good. It had obviously helped Jim, who had got the motors running the way he liked them, and done wonders for Ken and Julie who became engaged and, in fact, married shortly after the trip was over.

As medical officer I was in charge, of course, of all things medical. Alas, the only patient was me. In the Bilma Oasis, the furthermost point of our trek, I developed a pain which I recognised as a kidney stone. The whole expedition was laid up for a couple of days until I had recovered.

We were staying in the Oasis guest house, which was a mud hut with two iron bed frames. As the invalid, one of the bed frames was allotted to me, and the other to an American lady doctor in the party who was designated to look after me.

She was what is known as an abdominal angiographist (no such people exist in England – we can't afford them). Her sole medical duties in the U.S. were to illustrate with various radiological techniques, the different organs of the abdomen by squirting dyes up several unmentionable places.

She was nonplussed to be confronted with a real illness and it took a great deal of persuading to get her to give me a pain-relieving injection.

Our prolonged stay did mean that our group was invited to two parties by the local dignitaries; one for the group on its own, the second in the company of two astonishing American ladies.

A boxcar plane had landed on our second day in this isolated oasis. Out had stepped two immaculately groomed American women in spotless khaki bush jackets and skirts, notebooks in hand. They were representatives of the Diners Club who were looking for eating places in Africa to recommend to their company.

51

Not only had Bilma no eating places: you had to take your own food with you, otherwise you might go hungry. Because of my kidney stone I missed both parties. On the third day I passed my stone and, from being contorted in pain, I was suddenly completely better. This was fortunate, in more ways than one, as I was called to a native hut to treat two semi-conscious Niger airmen.

They'd been living it up on the local jungle juice the night before, I was told. Could I get them in some sort of shape?

I did what I could and to my horror, an hour later, I saw them being driven off back to the plane with our American Diners Club ladies – this was the aircrew that was going to fly them out.

They somehow got the plane off the ground and we watched it fly away into the distance. What could one wish them but *bon voyage* – and happy eating?

In later years uranium deposits were found in this area of Niger and – who knows? – you may well now be able to get a good meal in Bilma by passing a plastic card.

I was fortunate to see the Sahara at its best. Alas, I

understand that things have changed now. There's a tarmacadam road from Algiers to Tamanrasset and even in the beautiful, isolated Tenere Desert there are oil stations and oil rigs.

Touring companies are no longer able to do their own thing. If you do cross the Sahara you have to go in Algerian trucks with Algerian drivers, Algerian cooks and Algerian food. But, who can blame them? It's their country, after all.

CHAPTER 6

Two Loves

They say that it's possible to be in love with two women at the same time and I have to confess that, for most of my adult life and even during some of my schooldays, I have had two continuous and contemporaneous love affairs.

One has been with the River Thames and British Inland Waterways. The other has been with France.

As a family we have made various sporadic raids on Spain, Italy, Portugal, and I had a disastrous weekend in Austria, but to date we have found no good reason why we should go beyond France for our Continental holidays.

I first got to know the Thames during the war. When I was at school we would cycle up from south London to Folly Bridge in Oxford and hire one of Salter Brothers' camping rowing boats. The boats had three pairs of oars and metal hoops all the way down over which a canvas cover could be placed, just like *Three Men In a Boat*. The seats pulled out and mattresses pulled down. On two occasions during Easter holidays, we rowed the Thames, mooring on the bank at night and cooking our meals over wood fires. We had to be in bed by dark as there was a blackout, and we occasionally varied our spartan cooked diet by going into the local British restaurants in Wallingford and Goring.

Although I've grown too old for it now, this is the real way to travel on a river, with a pair of oars or a punt where you are down at water level and your progress is slow enough to take in everything that's going on. In later years, as regular visitors to the Thames in cabin cruisers, we've met boats similar to those of my schoolboy days with men in striped blazers and straw boaters, following the course of Jerome K. Jerome's intrepid trio. How I envy them.

Our first cruise was from Folly Bridge with Janice and Kevin Bird, when our children were too tiny to go boating. It was in the early Fifties and our boat was like an older sister of *The African Queen*, broken down more often than it was on the move.

Then one Easter, with Trevor about eleven, Paul nine and Jane a baby left in Zara's care, we went with a widow friend, Margaret Doe, and her daughter Sally, from Thames Ditton to Wallingford. We'd hired a 42ft Maid Line boat, in which Johnny Morris later made a film on the Thames.

We hadn't many of the modern amenities in those days. I remember Pam and I going to bed wearing every article of clothing we'd brought with us – two pairs of trousers, three sweaters, towels wrapped round our heads – and waking up in the morning to find icicles hanging like stalactites from the ceiling of our cabin.

Five or six years later, during a glorious summer, we took my mother and Jane, now old enough to come with us.

We had a scorching fortnight, travelling from Maidenhead up to Eynesham and back. It was so hot we often had to keep the boat moving just to get some breeze and stay cool.

On this particular trip Paul was just into fishing, and had brought along every possible bit of tackle available, all the right gear. Jane wanted to fish, too, so my mother put a bent pin on a piece of string and tied it to a bamboo rod. Jane pulled them out twice as fast as her expert fisherman brother.

Having a fortnight, we could take our journey at leisure. We visited Cookham, Marlow, Henley, Goring and Streatley. Trevor and I played golf at Hurley and I took Paul to see his first professional football match – Oxford v. Birmingham – and from then on Paul became a devoted Oxford United follower. He was faithful to Oxford until his move to Cirencester, when parenthood and distance stopped him. He'd become very involved with the team; in later years he used to write, for the Oxford United programme, match accounts and humorous stories which Gill illustrated.

There is no doubt that we got the most from the river on our trips with Lynne and Joe Church. They had given up jobs as teachers to live the good life in Devon. They grew their own vegetables, fished, prawned, lobstered and set up a hospital for injured birds of prey, such as sea hawks and kestrels.

Baby owls were brought to them as tiny little balls of fluff. Two that were so small that they could never learn to adjust to the wild life, and had to be kept on as pets.

Joe is the only man I've known who's had a love affair with an owl. It used to display for him and, even when it heard his car coming in the distance, used to get terribly excited. Alas, it was a male, so one had to conclude that it must have been gay.

Joe fought an almost losing battle to save the River Torridge in Devon which changed from an abundant salmon river to an almost dead river through the combination of effluent from various commercial enterprises, silage seeping from farms and, worst of all, almost untreated sewage pouring into the estuary.

He told me of one occasion when the authorities were trying to prove that the sewage effluent went out to sea by emptying boxes of oranges into the sewage wastefall and tracing their progress.

To their great surprise, half of the oranges landed upriver near Weir Gifford. He was bitter that millions of pounds were being spent on cleaning the Thames, resulting in salmon being caught up as far as Godstow Lock, whereas his own river at home was going progressively into decay.

When Lynne and Joe were aboard, they were always pointing out birds we didn't know, or lampreys and other unusual fish.

Walking along the towpath at Pangbourne one day, we found a live pike in the middle of the path. How on earth it got there I don't know. We thought it must have been charging after a small fish and got carried away, but there it was: not a fisherman in sight and a live four-pound pike lying at our feet. We managed to get it back safely into the river.

When we travelled on the Thames with Joe and Lynne we weren't trying to get from one point to another, we just ambled. But to most boat hirers the main achievement seemed to be distance – Oxford and back or Lechdale and back. Every boat had its throttle out to the full and they'd travel in packs from lock to lock. We cruised along, gently, perhaps having a pub lunch during the day. Pub lunches on the Thames are so inexpensive, it was almost cheaper eating out than on board.

At night we'd moor, out into the wild as far as possible from any other boat. Lynne's little border terrier, Jenny, and our Bertie would race off together. The dogs explored a thousand different smells along the bankside, rolling and tumbling in energetic doggy games.

Joe and Lynne were tremendous company.

I awoke one night to find the boat heeling over to port. My immediate thought was that the river level had fallen and our bank mooring ropes were holding one side up, whilst the other side had gone down with the falling water.

I yelled to Joe in the front cabin, 'We're heeling over! I'm going out on to the bank to check the mooring lines.'

A sleepy, 'I shouldn't worry, Skip,' was the only reply I got from Joe.

But I did worry. I got out of the boat in my pyjamas, got on to the bank flashed my torch. To my amazement, all the mooring lines were slack and the boat was riding on an even keel.

I climbed back on board and snuggled down into my sleeping bag. I just couldn't understand it.

At breakfast next morning Joe and Lynne had some obvious shared secret. They kept giggling and Lynne kept on saying 'Go on. Tell him, Joe.'

Eventually Joe, hardly containing his laughter said, 'It's like this Skip . . .' (For Joe to call me Skip was incongruous, as he had a full beard on his face that was the spitting image of the sailor on the old Players cigarette packets.) 'You know Lynne bought a new dress in Abingdon yesterday? Apparently I didn't take much notice of it.

'Well, she only buys a dress about once every hundred years and was very upset about my lack of interest. She was so upset that I climbed over and joined her in her bunk to comfort her. It gave the boat a bit of a list. That's when you jumped out to check the moorings. We were laughing so much, seeing you on the bank in your pyjamas, that we decided to put off any more comforting until we get back to Devon.'

He roared with laughter, knocking his teacup over Lynne. Lynne jumped up as the hot water splashed over her, sending all the breakfast things crashing to the floor.

'You're a clumsy oaf, Joe Church!' she said, mopping herself with a tea towel.

'You're going to have to comfort her again, Joe,' I said. 'But, as Captain of this ship, I order in future that all comforting be confined to the river bank. The Skipper must get his sleep even if the crew don't.'

Still, the mystery was solved. The keeling-over did not join the *Marie Celeste* as one of the great unsolved riddles of our time.

With a friend, Pam Knowles, Pam and I once went up the

Oxford Canal in a fibreglass boat as far as Rugby. The canal had some beautiful spots, but so much of it could be improved: silted-up stretches, overgrown and crumbling banks, faulty locks. With three million unemployed in Britain, you would think there could be some way of directing energies towards improving facilities such as this.

This particular holiday was distinguished by the fact that it rained without stopping. The toilet arrangements on the boat were very inadequate and I spent a lot of my time crouched behind hedges under an umbrella answering nature's calls. We were more than pleased to get home. The holiday coincided with Wimbledon Fortnight and I think the tennis fans had an even worse time than we did.

We had canal holidays, too, going up the Severn, along the Stratford and Worcester Canal to Kinver. The beautiful and unique Brecon Abergavenny Canal runs along the Usk Valley where time seems to have stood still. Villages along the canal seem to be back in the Twenties, both in looks and prices. I remember getting marvellous meat pasties for 10p each, and four of us dining with a bottle of wine for about £6 – this was only about ten years ago.

Our ambition was that one day, perhaps when we'd retired, we would live on the Thames and have a boat moored at the bottom of the garden. We would also have liked to have retired to France. Whenever we went on holiday, too – as the children kept reminding us – we always wanted to buy a cottage where we had stayed. I'm glad we never did because it would have tied us to one spot. It's much easier to go and hire somewhere with a new area to explore, not having responsibilities of owning and main-taining a property.

The more we went on the Thames, the more we liked it. We used to manage a trip most years. Although at one time it seemed that the river would become choked with boats, in later years they actually started to reduce in number. Boating is not a cheap holiday and the English weather is unpredictable. The Thames is not always predictable, either, as we found to our cost when it flooded and we were stuck at Sonning Lock for a few days.

It's much cheaper to get a package holiday and it's easier on the mums: food is prepared, and mums get a rest from the cooking and washing up. But it's not nearly so much fun for the rest of us.

*　　*　　*

Our first camping trip to the Continent was with Kevin and Janice Bird to Spain. Then came the first one with the children when, in a Volkswagen Dormobile, we also took Pam's father, Jerry down to the South of France. You could say Jerry was a late starter: he began his camping/caravanning life at the age of 75.

From then on, as a family, we criss-crossed France, sometimes going to Italy – usually making for the Mediterranean – but camping all over the Dordogne, Brittany, the Jura Mountains, and most often in the real heart of France itself; in small unknown places with municipal campsites by a river. Often we were the only English family on the site, and became part of the camping community – our children mixing with children from Sweden, Holland, Denmark, Belgium, Germany, France and Spain. Somehow, as children do, they all managed to communicate, in no way hindered by speaking different languages.

It was a great sadness to me when the children grew up and started to go on their own holidays: Trevor to see actor friends in New York; Jane to Poros in the Greek islands, to be followed home by a stream of letters and telephone calls from a Greek barman with the first letter headed, 'Well, what do you think of we Greece boys?' Paul and Gill toured with friends in the Dordogne and Cognac country.

Pam and I did a fly-drive from Lyons, exploring the Drôme area of France, staying in the delightful town of Crest, then crossing the Rhône Valley up through the Ardèche to the spa of Vals les Bains.

At Vals les Bains, we were shown around the spa, where the patients were having mud baths and being hosed down. I think spa treatment is a much under-used branch of medicine. Many of the therapies, analysed, don't offer much clinical help, but there's no doubt that most of the procedures made people come out feeling better. That, I've always felt, is the basic purpose of the practice of medicine.

We then travelled south and down to Arles. As it was out of season, we had the amphitheatre and coliseum to ourselves. We crossed to the busy, crowded Avignon, a lovely university town where the students seemed to spend their time sitting around having coffee. Next we headed north, up to Orange, again to have the place to ourselves and enjoy a leisurely procession through the triumphal arch.

The last night we spent in Vienne, where I'd played rugby in 1947 and where we were thrashed 47–3 by the local side. I tried in the hotel to find out if anybody remembered us but nobody did – it was a long time ago – although they still had a good rugby team in the town itself.

*   *   *

With the arrival of Daisy May, our first granddaughter, the whole holiday cycle with children began again.

Paul and Gill loved France. Paul, given an opportunity, would go and live there. As he travelled on business in his car he would play language cassettes to improve his French, just in case his firm decided to open a branch out there.

We wanted to find somewhere convenient in France so that we could perhaps rent an appartment and the children and grandchildren could come over and see us. We might even have the chance of keeping grandchildren to ourselves for a spell.

We decided that it would have to be in Normandy or Brittany, so we went off on two short holidays of exploration. We had six days of being driven round by our neighbours, Stan and Pauline Williams, in their Range Rover. It was the first time I'd ever been on the Continent and not been the driver, though I think navigating was almost as difficult. The great advantage of a Range Rover is that you are that much higher and see so much more of the countryside. We crossed from

Portsmouth to Cherbourg in September in very uncertain weather, landing up near the Pegasus Bridge for our first night.

We saw what looked like quite a smart motel and, on enquiring about the cost of a room, I thought the receptionist said *soixante-cinq* i.e. 65 francs. I marvelled at the price, because this was such splendid accommodation.

'Are you sure there isn't a *cent* – a hundred – mixed in there somewhere?' Stan asked. Later we discovered that he was absolutely right – there was a hundred mixed in. The rooms were 650 francs – £70 – a night.

It was complete luxury: we'd never stayed in such opulence. There were peach-coloured dressing gowns hung behind the bathroom door, bowls of fruit on the table, and we had the most enormous and expensive dinner. We had hoped to start with mussels, which were on the menu, but they were off that night. Instead we got raw sardines in milk with apples. Then masses of ham in cider with cauliflower cheese. Already we were just about filled to our eyebrows. We passed on the next dish which was going to be toasted cheese and opted for a patisserie, hoping for a little bit of local apple tart.

When they brought the flambé trolley our patisserie proved to be a baked apple on pastry, crêpes cooked at the table, placed on the apple then covered with massive amounts of cream and calvados. Then the whole thing was set alight.

I spent the whole night sitting upright in bed with horrific indigestion.

The hotel was obviously aimed at the American market – people came over to visit the many graveyards near the old battle areas there – but it was good value for money.

This most expensive restaurant, which we thought would be pretty empty, eventually finished full. It was rather disappointing for me, with such splendour, wonderful dishes, immaculate waiters and waitresses, that only Stan and I were in a collar and tie. The rest of these international diners were in jumpers and open necked shirts. It somehow took the edge off things.

We saw Deauville, which disappointed us. But we loved
Torville, another seaside resort, that had originally been made
popular by *les Anglais*. Then we motored without stopping
through Lisieux down to our next planned stop at Bagnoles-de-
l'Orne, a beautiful little spa town with a lake and, nearby, a
huge spa centre with 30 hotels grouped round it.

We stayed at a very nice hotel just by the lake. Walking into
the town we had a first-class meal for £6 or £7, a fraction of what
we'd paid the night before.

We had two days there and, unexpectedly, we'd brought the
sunshine with us. Having two nights in Bagnoles-de-l'Orne, we
were able to picnic and travel round, visiting Domfront and
Mortain, then on to Dinard where I'd booked us into the
Grand. We'd started this as an expensive holiday, I thought –
let's finish it with a flourish.

The Grand is a beautiful old hotel overlooking the bay at
Dinard with St. Malo the other side of the bay. There was
always something happening: busy little fishing boats going
out, the ferries leaving St. Malo, literally hundreds of sailing
boats and motor launches, all in wonderful sunshine. We took
the ferry across to St. Malo and walked round its outer walls.

They had all been knocked down during the war, but were now re-built exactly as they used to be 300 or 400 years ago. The narrow streets opened up into cafe areas, enabling us to sit in the sunshine, drinking cups of coffee and watching people walk by.

The Grand at Dinard is a lovely old hotel, created by our Victorian forefathers: great big old-fashioned rooms, views over the bay, lovely dining rooms, lounges, a very smart restaurant with reasonably priced food for the type of hotel. But again, there was hardly anyone in a collar and tie.

There was a course or convention for economics students going on. The students, dining in these surroundings in jeans and open shirts somehow didn't fit. Perhaps it showed how old-fashioned I was.

We called in at Dinan on the way back, had coffee down by the River Rance, then home by ferry. Just to show how small the world is, on the ferry we bumped into seven people we knew well. I said to Pam, 'You can't take your mistress anywhere nowadays.'

Once home, we were eager to get back to France to explore further. We thought that probably Dinard was the best area to get an apartment: by car it's only three and a half hours from Cherbourg. There's a night boat to St. Malo from Portsmouth and then either a ferry across to Dinard, or a short journey round by car to meet the boat.

We set off for a four-day trip with a doctor friend and his wife from Berkshire, Jim and Tighe Reeves. We spent a night in Portsmouth, crossing to Cherbourg and then driving down along the coast to spend our first night at the beautiful fishing port of Honfleur. We would have loved to have stayed longer in Honfleur. It's a picture postcard sort of place but, like most French coastal towns, busy with fishing boats coming in and out and a dredger working in the harbour.

We had one night there. Next day we went for coffee and shopping in Lisieux. Then we went for a picnic to a spot we'd found in the wood near Bagnoles when we'd been with Stan and Pauline, finishing our day in Dinard.

This was October and most of the hotels were shut. We didn't make for the Majestic or the Grand, but looked for something less pricey and found a marvellous hotel right on the shoreline. The Hotel de la Vallée was a third of the price of the Grand, had excellent food and accommodation, with the waves virtually lapping at the door and fishing boats landing their catch outside.

We'd been lucky with our weather in September; we were even luckier with our weather in October. It was hotter still.

The passenger ferry was closed down by now, so we had to go to St. Malo to the hypermarket by car for the girls to shop and the men to buy our wine. Small world again – Jim bumped into one of his patients in the hypermarket.

We found a splendid apartment at Residence Hoteliere Les Pins in Dinard which we booked for a month for the last half of May and the beginning of June for the next year. It would hold six, so we hoped to have the children and friends over for short bursts with us, as well as ourselves going off further into Brittany. We forget that France is such a big country, with so much to explore.

I don't forget that England is beautiful. In fact, I don't think there is a more beautiful country. If only we could be guaranteed sunshine, I'd probably not travel at all.

CHAPTER 7

I Nearly Went to . . .

I still went occasionally to London to broadcast for a BBC magazine programme. After one such programme there was a party for somebody leaving. We all became quite merry and one of the young and very presentable presenters, Mary, was looking for somebody to go with her to Moscow the following October.

The producer of the programme couldn't; apparently he was *persona non grata* behind the Iron Curtain. I don't know whether it was one drink too many, but suddenly on the train home I realised that I'd promised to escort a young, nubile and very attractive BBC presenter for a few days in Moscow.

Mary was a great girl with a good sense of humour so I sat down and wrote her a very careful letter saying that to travel hopefully is better than to arrive. Anticipation is all. Taken to its logical conclusion, it is even better to not set off at all, merely nearly to go somewhere. The relevant part of the letter, which I reckon is very sound advice, read:

Every year we hear that more and more people go on holiday. Five million to Spain, seven million to Blackpool or wherever. Going away has its hazards: one is exposed to all sorts of new diseases, muggings, hijacking, food poisoning, as well as spending considerable amounts of money.

One of the very much neglected arts, in a society which neglects most of its art, is the art of nearly going somewhere. A planned resurgence of this art could help restore both mental and economic stability to this country and it is an effective counter-inflationary method.

Nearly going somewhere is not as simple as it might look. I am at present nearly going to Moscow next October with a lady I met at a party. If you are nearly going to go somewhere it's not enough merely to carry the thought in your mind. You have to make the same planned approach as if you're organising some bona fide holiday, be it in England or on the Continent.

Carelessness can cause havoc. For example: it's no use preparing nearly to go somewhere with an out-of-date passport: the situation could arise when you might actually have to go somewhere and need a valid passport. Not only would you not be able to appreciate nearly going to the place in future, but you might get the sack as well. So it's best to have two passports: one for show and one for blow. The ideal second passport for the practitioner of the art is a surrendered one with the corner clipped off which everybody knows is no use at all.

It's no use going to a travel agency for up-to-date brochures. You must search the back of your desk for last year's brochures where obsolete dates and prices are quoted, but which include all the anticipatory blurb to whet your appetite about the place you're nearly going to.

The best time to arrange to nearly go away is when you have some prior commitment. If you want nearly to go to Paris, for example, try and fix a date which you know will coincide with your admission to hospital for the removal of your gall bladder.

The main benefits of nearly going somewhere are the saving of money and the preserving of friendship. It's on holiday that you most often quarrel with your friends and on holiday that you spend more money than usual.

Nowadays there is the additional benefit that if you never leave your back garden, the chances of being held hostage by an Arab hijacker are very small indeed.

An added bonus is if you can persuade someone to pair with you in the pursuit of this art. If, for example, you are able to say, 'Jimmy Saville and I nearly went to Majorca last year', not only will you be accepted at any party, but all your colleagues will be in awe of you.

Nearly going somewhere has been a tradition in my family and it's been a matter of family honour when planning nearly to go somewhere to go about it industriously. It brings many fringe benefits; now I have an aunt who says she was nearly on the *Titanic*; my grandfather says he was nearly in the San Francisco earthquake and, more recently, my eldest nephew was nearly in the Mediterranean when a ship was hijacked. Most of our family folklore is based on situations when members of the family were nearly present, and it is only by diligent bookkeeping that they've been able to show how very near they were to being there.

Finally, for the person who decides he is nearly going somewhere, 100 per cent physical fitness is essential. Regular exercise, clean living, abstinence from smoking and consumption of alcohol and regular medical check-ups will ensure this. Unless you're actually fit enough nearly to go somewhere, there's no point in nearly going somewhere at all.

I posted my letter to Mary on a Monday, expecting a fairly amusing reply. However, I had a phone call on Wednesday from John, producer of the magazine programme. 'We want you to take part in a live broadcast on Sunday,' he said.

'I can't get up to London,' I replied, quite excited about the thought of the broadcast.

'You don't have to worry about that,' said John. 'I've fixed for you to be linked in from an unmanned station.' He named a place near Winchcombe that I'd never heard of, not realising that the BBC had these places.

'What's the programme about?' I asked.

'You're going to be hoisted by your own petard,' said John. 'Doctor Robert Clifford will read his piece on "The Art of Nearly Going Somewhere". You've got to be careful when you write to us.'

The following Sunday I made my way up to a strange place, some sort of listening post for people who monitor foreign broadcasts. Everybody walked around as if they still had their headphones on. I reported at the desk and was met by a huge man who seemed upset that his Sunday was being disturbed. He marched me off into a bungalow next door. The lounge of this bungalow was an actual little broadcasting studio equipped with a few switchboards.

I sat down to wait, wearing a pair of headphones and listening to a programme. My escort sat down to read the Sunday paper. Suddenly over the headphones came a voice: 'Are you there, Doctor Clifford? This is John here. You'll be on in five minutes.'

It was all very disorientating. I could hear the programme rattling along, and then came John's voice: 'Hello, Doctor

Clifford, down in the West Country. How are things there?' I replied with some non-committal phrase. 'Good – and now we'd all like to hear about this new art you've devised of nearly going somewhere.'

I then read the letter I'd written for Mary. There was a sort of 'Thank you' in my headphones, then dead silence in the room as the programme was cut off. It was very strange: I didn't know whether I'd been broadcasting or not.

'Was that all right,' I asked my escort.

'I suppose so,' he said, not having listened to a word of it. He rattled his keys, impatient to be off, and I came away with a very weird feeling. I'd been talking into space and I couldn't believe that thousands, perhaps even millions, had been listening to me talking to myself in this bungalow. Anyway, back home I'd see what Pam thought.

'What did you think of the broadcast, then?'

'What broadcast?' she said. 'I thought you'd just gone for a rehearsal.'

I rang my secretary, whom I'd instructed to listen.

'What did you think of my broadcast?'

'I don't know,' she said. 'It was all in French.' She'd obviously got the wrong programme.

I now was really disorientated. I'd been sitting in the bungalow thinking I was giving a broadcast. Had *anybody* heard it? I walked out to the garden to collect my thoughts and there was Stan Williams trimming his roses along the fence.

'Are you nearly going to do some gardening, Bob?' he asked.

All was well, it *had* been broadcast. I don't know how many people listened to the programme, but I might have started a new art. I could quite easily be the head of some new culture. Or I might nearly . . .

CHAPTER 8

Achilles Heel

There's no doubt that marriage is a lottery, and in my marriage I won a top prize. Pam is all the things a wife should be: loving, patient, caring, supportive, tolerant. People say we've achieved the perfect balance: she gives and I take.

She's the nicest lady I've ever met. Putting up with me has proved that.

I was always bombarding her with visitors, sometimes at very short notice. My second son, Paul, has inherited this trait. This was most obvious when he had his rock group and was hoping to emulate the Beatles.

A few minutes before a meal he'd arrive with three friends, saying, 'Is it all right if they stay and eat with us?' Paul had even less insight into the preparation of meals than I did.

Pam was almost unflappable. She had though, like everybody else, her Achilles heel, just one small area of vulnerability which, when affected, would cause all the calm to disappear.

She liked to have her furniture in exactly the same rooms and kept in exactly the same position as she put it. If I moved an armchair from one side of the room to another it would bring her almost to a state of frenzy.

The only other thing that would upset her was a story I continually told against her.

I would say, 'If I walked in with a beautiful young woman and said, "Oh, Pam, I met this nice young woman from the *Folies Bergère* and I asked her back for the night," Pam's reaction would be, "Oh dear. I wish you'd let me know sooner and I would have put clean sheets on the bed." Whereas if I moved my favourite armchair from one side of the room to the other, one would have thought World War Three had broken out.'

She didn't like me telling this story, nor did she like me moving furniture.

Over a period of time, Pam seemed to get quieter and less interested in what I did. There was a flurry of the old spirit when I said, 'Les Hoyle asked would we like an old desk?' She then gave a spirited monologue about not wanting old desks.

It was a most beautiful old rolltop inlaid mahogany desk, which had secret drawers and a writing pad full of quills. It was a very valuable piece of furniture, so I accepted it and took it upstairs, hiding it in my study.

Pam didn't mind, providing she couldn't see it. I used it as a work desk for some time, but suddenly realised that it was more than probably the most valuable piece of furniture in the house. Rather than be left in my darkened study, it would look much better in our lounge, although admittedly it would take up a fair amount of room.

Pam was now much more into this disinterested state and I wondered whether she was getting depressed. I thought that suddenly she looked older.

Plucking up all my courage I broached the subject of my desk. 'Look, darling,' I said, 'the most valuable piece of furniture we have in the house is my desk in the study. I think we should have it in the lounge. It's very ornamental and it would be better looked after downstairs.'

'If that's what you want,' Pam said, 'fine,' and went on reading a book.

Without wasting a moment in case she changed her mind, I

shot upstairs with Paul. The two of us managed to get the desk down and assembled in the front lounge, where it looked really good.

Pam appeared not even to notice it was there and seemed to get progressively slower and continued losing interest in things generally.

I had a good look at her one evening and it seemed as if she'd aged even in the last month. Suddenly something clicked at the back of my mind – Myxoedema. This means you're short of thyroid. It's an insidious condition, very slow in onset, a bit like a gramophone slowly winding down. People who are short of thyroid often lose the outer third of their eyebrows. Pam hadn't, but very often this is a diagnostic factor. You also get some skin changes and hair changes, and can become constipated. I found she'd put on weight and there were one or two other little physical signs.

73

We did some blood tests, and Pam's thyroid proved to be very much underactive. An underactive thyroid is one of the easiest conditions to treat. All it means is taking some thyroid tablets to make up for the thyroid hormone you're not producing, and over a few months you start firing on all cylinders again.

Your hair becomes soft, your skin becomes smoother, you have twice as much energy, you feel better, you lose weight and, as they say, you become more regular.

The day after the first thyroid tablet, Pam suddenly felt quite light-headed and much more alive. After about a couple of months she was back to her old self again, full of energy. It was a joy to have her back as she'd always been.

A few months later we were sitting in the lounge when Pam suddenly looked up and asked, 'What's that desk doing there?'

'It's been there for the last four months,' I said. 'You didn't mind me bringing it down.'

'Good God,' she said. 'I must have been ill. Anyway, now it's here, I expect it can stay: it does look quite nice.'

Just to test she had fully recovered, I switched all the armchairs into different positions in the lounge after Pam had gone to bed. I shot off to work early, and came back at lunchtime to find her furious. 'What do you mean?' she said. 'Changing everything round when I'm not there? Just because you got away with the desk, don't think you're going to get away with everything.'

I was completely reassured. 'It's all right, darling,' I said. 'I was just seeing whether you were on the right dose of thyroid tablets.'

'You monkey,' she said. 'I had a feeling it was something like that – but don't you dare try it again or I'll stop your egg sandwiches.'

Egg sandwiches are part of the family folklore. When I got married I was a nine-stone wonder, but after five years I'd gone from nine to about 14 stone. I attributed this to the egg sandwiches that Pam made so beautifully. Unless I stopped Pam's tablets, there was no chance of my sneaking any desks or

74

any other furniture in without Pam's full approval – not in the face of a threat like that.

*　　*　　*

It wasn't only Pam who was found to have an illness. I had recovered well from a coronary bypass operation of three years ago, but five months after the operation I contracted a virus infection.

I kept it at bay with lots of fluid and plenty of aspirin. I managed to keep on working, knowing that if I stopped at this stage I might never start again.

It left me, I think due to the aspirin, with more indigestion than I usually have. I've always been a bit prone to indigestion and was suspicious that I had a condition called hiatus hernia. This is a very common condition and it's thought that 60 or 70 per cent of the population suffer from it.

It means that the valve at the top of the stomach is weak to varying degrees. Acid, which can happily live in the stomach, splashes the lower end of the gullet and burns it. With a hiatus hernia, you're likely to have some problems when you're bending forward or lying down.

Stomach complaints are usually investigated by two procedures. The first is a barium meal, in which you swallow some white stuff, which is photographed as it goes down. The other is a gastroscopy, in which a tube with a light on the end is pushed down your gullet to examine your stomach and duodenum.

Gastroscopes are marvellous instruments nowadays, narrow and flexible. Everybody I knew who had had one said a gastroscopy was nothing, but I – who had always had a bit of trouble swallowing even pills – developed almost a phobia at the very thought of it.

One of the unpleasant symptoms of hiatus hernia is that sometimes, at night, acid will come up into your mouth, turn down towards your lungs and make you cough – very unpleasant and quite frightening. One of the factors that make all this more likely is weight and I'd started to creep up from the 12½ stone that I was after the coronary bypass to 14 stone.

The barium X-ray showed just what I thought it would – a hiatus hernia with a bit of what is known as a reflux œsophagus, i.e. acid coming up and splashing the gullet. I put myself on a slimming regime, but failed to lose any weight. I'm not a big meal-eater, but I do like the odd sandwich, piece of cake, biscuit and, if nobody's looking, bar of chocolate.

John Bowler, consultant physician at Winchcombe Hospital, encouraged me to have a gastroscopy. 'You haven't completed your investigation,' he said. 'Until this is done, anything could be happening.'

Even though I'd been through a very major operation without much trouble, this particular procedure I was attempting to avoid at all costs.

I tried everything I knew to be a physician curing himself, but my stomach got worse rather than better. Eventually I gave in to John Bowler's pushing and agreed to go and see a gastroenterologist in Winchcombe, Eric Crew. He was a

delightful man to whom I'd sent many patients. He gave me a good looking-over, examined my barium meal reports, showed me that for some reason my stomach was standing on its side instead of lying down, which he said was probably due to fat, and talked about high-fibre diets.

Just when I thought I'd got away with it, he said, 'But of course, we must do a gastroscopy to make sure there's nothing else going on.' He arranged for one to be done two days later.

I spent the next 48 hours making my will and putting my affairs in order, which was absolutely stupid. I'd sent dozens of patients for this procedure and none of them had complained. They said they didn't even know it'd been done – particularly when Eric was doing it – but I was convinced I'd be the first GP to die from a gastroscopy.

At the hospital they gave me a jab in my rear quarters as a pre-medication. Then Eric sprayed a local anaesthetic in the back of my throat and said, 'Now I'm going to give you a little injection to put you into Happy Land.' He injected something into my arm and I felt pleasantly drowsy. Just before this injection I'd had to grip something like a serviette ring in my mouth in case I clenched my teeth. In this pleasant drowsy state I could vaguely feel something happening in my throat. The next thing I knew was Eric saying. 'I've finished now. You can get up, have a cup of tea in half an hour, and then go home.

'All's well. You've just got a bit of hiatus hernia with some reflux and inflammation at the lower end of the gullet. Follow the diet and I'll see you in six months.'

It was all over – and I'd hardly felt a thing.

What children we men are! Just the fact that there was nothing nasty going on almost cured me on the spot. I stuck to Eric's regime, started knocking off weight, ate plenty of bran took some tablets he'd prescribed and from the great lump of fat I'd become, a svelte figure began to emerge. Even better – my indigestion started to disappear.

CHAPTER 9

Fishing Dangerously

Now and again I would get three days off in a row. It was not enough time to get away any distance, but enough for three consecutive days' fishing on the River Tad.

Three days' fishing I found ideal. There was time enough for the weather to change after a bad start; time for a sudden shower to freshen up the water in a hot spell; for sulking fish to come back on the feed; for another run of sea trout; for a new hatch of flies on the water; time to explore new swims when familiar ones proved unproductive; to observe and predict the changes in flow and water level.

By the end of three days I'd usually had enough fishing for the time being, without my interest starting to flag. And there was a lot to talk about afterwards in the Tadchester Arms with John Denton.

John was the water bailiff on the Tad, an expatriate Mancunian for whom the job was more than just a living: he ate, drank and slept fish and fishing; knew every hole and eddy along the river.

He was enormously patient with the junior anglers, quietly coaching them in the proper way to fish, and teaching them the respect they should show to their catch and the wildlife of the waterside.

He was not quite so patient with adult anglers he caught cheating, poaching, ill-treating their catch, or littering or damaging the banks. He would give them the benefit of the doubt and let them off the first time with a warning. But if he caught them a second time, then they seldom tried it a third. John was a big lad.

During my three-day sessions, he would join me on the bank for a couple of hours, morning and evening, making sure that I knocked off in the mornings at twelve noon for a break. Twelve noon was the time when the fish stopped biting or, to put it another way, when John knocked off for his lunchtime pint in the Tadchester Arms. The fish miraculously came back on feed at closing time.

I was glad to have John with me on the first day of a session in early March. We were fishing the Tad from a field in which grazed a herd of about twenty bullocks. They were some distance from us and behaving as bullocks usually do: quietly munching the grass and generally mooning about. But something was worrying John. Every so often he would glance over his shoulder at the herd, whose grazing pattern was bringing them slowly closer.

'What's the matter, John?' I asked. 'Bullocks are harmless, surely?'

'Normally, yes. But you mustn't trust 'em too far. I'm keeping my eye on that big bugger there: the one that's making a nuisance of himself.'

One of the bullocks was nudging and butting his neighbours; sometimes playfully, but sometimes as if he meant it. The recipients of the butting simply snorted in protest and moved away, at which the big bullock would turn on another victim.

The disturbance was speeding up the animals' natural movements towards the river and the herd was about 30 yards from us when John muttered, 'Hey up, our Bob! Look at that.'

I looked over my shoulder to see the big bullock attempting to mount one of its comrades, who kicked up his heels and lumbered off.

'That thing hasn't had a proper job done on him,' said John. 'As a bull he might not be up to much, but a straightforward bullock he isn't.'

The creature swung round, presenting its hindquarters to us. There, between its legs, swung a modestly sized, lopsided but unmistakable scrotum. The castration pincers may have accounted for half its potential, but they'd obviously left the other half intact.

Some further inexpert and unsuccessful attempts at mounting its fellows left the bullock in a temper. After galloping around the herd a couple of times, it moved down towards the river. Ten yards from us it stopped, squinted shortsightedly, lowered its head and sniffed, then snorted and pawed the ground.

'Do just as I say, Bob,' said John in a hoarse whisper. 'Get up slowly and walk backwards towards that gate in the hedge. Leave the tackle where it is and keep your eyes on me laddo there.'

Both of us stood up slowly and started walking backwards.

John quietly unzipped his anorak.

'Take yours off as well, Bob,' he hissed. 'Behind your back. And no sudden movements.'

'OK, John,' I hissed back. (Hissing seems to be catching.) 'But what for?'

'I'll give you the word when to run. If the bugger gets too close, throw your anorak over your shoulder. He'll stop to toss it around for a bit.'

The bullock walked, snorting, to our baskets on the bank and tipped both over with sideways scoops of its horns. Then it lifted its head, fixed us with bloodshot eyes, and broke into a lumbering trot.

'Right, Bob!' yelled John. 'RUN!'

We turned and ran. Both of us breaking records for a hundred-yard sprint over tussocky pasture. Behind us we heard the pounding of hooves, speeding up and gaining rapidly.

I was just about to throw my anorak, reluctantly, over my

shoulder when I reached the gate. How I'd got so quickly to a
point so far away I'll never know. There were two almost
simultaneous thuds as John and I vaulted the gate and landed
heavily on the other side.

The bullock skidded to a stop, rattled the bars of the gate
angrily with butts and scoops of its horns, then lost interest and
lumbered back to annoy the herd again.

'Thank God we kept the Country Code,' puffed John. 'If we'd left that gate open we'd be looking like something from the last reel of *Blood and Sand* by now. I see you didn't use your anorak, by the way. Didn't fancy a bit of the old corrida, then?'

'To tell the truth,' I said, 'it's a present from Pam. First time I've worn it. Even as a fishing story it would sound a bit far-fetched – my new anorak ripped to bits in a bullfight. Why didn't you use yours?'

'It's got all the tools of my trade in the pockets: credentials as bailiff, books and permits, copies of the byelaws and Water Authority regulations. If they got scattered to the four winds I'd be lost. What's a bailiff without his rule books? Besides, as a story it's like yours – who the hell would believe it?'

We picked ourselves up, dusted ourselves off, and were debating whether it was safe to go back and retrieve our tackle, when a crusty old farmer appeared, waving a knobbly walking stick.

'Hoi!' he bellowed. 'You annoying my cattle?'

When the old farmer got close enough, he recognised John, who explained about the bullock. To save possible future damage to anglers and the rest of the herd – but with the rest of the herd mainly in mind – the farmer promised an early appointment for the brute with a hamburger parlour.

The farmer was not exactly keen on anglers. The previous year he'd had a couple of bored and drunken anglers waving jackets at his bullocks in bullfighting passes, shouting '*Toro!*' and '*Arriba!*', and threatening to deliver the *coup de grâce* with rod rests.

'Running all the meat off my stock,' he muttered. 'Drunken buggers. I fixed 'em, though.'

'What with?' I asked. Naively.

'Two barrels of a twelve-bore in the arse of their pants,' he chuckled. 'Never did come back for their tackle. Made a fair bit out o' that, I did.'

. . .'Well, that was enough excitement for one morning, John,' I said, taking the top off a pint in the Tadchester Arms. 'I thought fishing was supposed to be relaxing. An aid to peace of mind, longevity and all that.'

'So it is, in between being in peril of your life,' said John. 'Did you know that in 1982 angling killed more people in Britain than any other single sport or leisure activity?'

'Get away.'

'True. Eleven anglers went to the Great Match Peg in the Sky. Ten by drowning. Official Census Office figures, those are. But it's not that bad, really. Angling's bigger than all the other participant sports put together. Eleven out of three million anglers isn't a lot. Much safer than crossing the road. Or getting stung by a bee.'

'I'm glad to hear it, John. But, come to think of it, the first time I met you professionally was when you came to the surgery with a damn great treble hook in your backside. The second time was when a pike minced your finger.' John winced at the memory of the treble hook, put into him by a cack-handed novice angler, and again at the memory of the pike's teeth. 'And you've put a fair few patients my way since, from accidents on the river.'

'Right,' he said. 'And I've sent a fair few more straight up to Casualty at Winchcombe Hospital. You've not seen the half of 'em, Bob. But mainly, thank God, they're small accidents. Nothing serious. Most of 'em are stupid, like that hook I copped for. And like the old boys who flake out with a heart attack as soon as they hook a big fish. But some of them are downright weird.'

'Weird?'

'Weird. Who would believe that a cow could fall on anybody, for a start?'

'Go on, John. I'll buy it. How could a cow fall on anybody?'

'From the top of the bank. The cow grazed right to the edge, slipped and fell right on a bloke fishing at the bottom. Good job it landed on its feet, or he'd have been dead. But its legs were straddled wide and it couldn't get up. All you could see of this bloke was his wellies, sticking out from underneath. He couldn't even shout for help, not with his head under a damn great udder. Luckily there were a few of us around who heard the crash.

83

'It took six of us to get the cow on its feet. And then it had the cheek to lift its tail and flop all over the bloke's face. I've heard of a pat on the back, but this was ridiculous. I told him it was good for the complexion, but he didn't seem too thrilled.'

John was in his stride now, and for the next hour I listened to a steady stream of bizarre events that normally happen only in *Carry On* films.

One angler, bending over his tackle box, was butted into the Tad by a sexed-up ram. In the tupping season, even the supposedly harmless sheep can't be trusted.

Another angler had to be sent for specialised treatment in London after being bitten by a tiny and innocent-looking lamb.

He contracted a rare and dangerous condition called *orf*. Orf must have been endemic around Tadchester: it was the second case I'd heard of in my time there.

Swans are notorious for their viciousness towards anglers. Anglers are notorious for their viciousness towards swans, so perhaps they cancel each other out. John, whose duties as bailiff were towards both anglers and swans, swore he kept an open mind.

'But *geese*,' he said. 'Geese are something else. You get swans one, two, three or four at a time. Geese you get in gaggles, and if you get a gaggle around your groundbait, you might just as well pack up and go home. Look at that poor girl last summer.'

'What poor girl last summer?'

'Not one of your patients, Bob. Winchcombe job, this was. She was with her boyfriend walking along the river bank, feeding the ducks and generally messing about. Wearing a short skirt. She bent down to pick up a crust she'd dropped, and didn't notice the geese behind her . . .'

He paused for a swig of his pint.

'Go on, John. The suspense is killing me.'

'Bloody near killed her as well. She bent over, presenting a perfect target, and she was goosed by the gander. Before she could draw breath, about half a dozen geese got into the act. I ran her and her boyfriend in my Land Rover over to Winchcombe where they diagnosed multiple abrasions and galloping hysteria. She didn't half carry on. I bet she's worn brass knickers ever since.'

You have to forgive John. Now and again he lowers the tone.

It's a fact, however, that farm animals attracted by groundbait or sandwiches can get very short tempered when the angler tries to dissuade them. One angler on the Tad was bitten by a goat. The resultant swelling put his casting arm out of action for a fortnight. Another was bitten by a pig, from which he contracted a nasty dose of swine fever. Several were savaged because they put a hand into a bucket of groundbait and failed to notice the rat having a free meal inside. (Anybody who thinks a rat is not a farm animal should spend a week on the average farm.)

Nightfishers often get a nasty fright when a wandering cow blunders into their tent. Others have their tent collapse around them when the cow decides that it makes a handy scratching post.

Bullocks – even successfully treated bullocks, unlike the half-equipped freak which chased us – can sometimes turn frisky, if not nasty, and do a fair bit of goring, butting, squashing and trampling.

Horses are often the culprits. One bunch of young anglers had to take to the water when a horse ate their lunches – even down to the pork pies – crunched their beer cans with its teeth, swigged the contents, and then attacked them with flailing hooves. The teenage lads, up to their waists in water, felt thoroughly ashamed of themselves when a tiny girl ran down to the river with a bridle, scolded the horse soundly and led it quietly away.

Exposure and hypothermia are common, either because anglers fail to dress properly, or sit for too long in windy stretches of the water. Another cause is the duckings, to which even the most agile and sober angler is occasionally prone.

'But most of the duckings happen in the afternoon,' said John, 'when the lads have overdone things a bit in the Tadchester Arms. The trouble then is that often they don't feel the cold. They'll carry on fishing soaking wet.

'The worst case of hypothermia I've heard of, though, happened nowhere near the water. Poor old Sid Williams, it was, early last December. The "ding-dong-merrilys" had already begun at the Tadchester Anglers' clubhouse. Sid got well tanked up there one night and two of his mates had to take him home.

'With friends like that you don't need enemies. The cowards just propped him against the door at midnight, rang the bell and ran away.'

'I bet he got into trouble with his wife,' I said.

'Not straightaway. His wife didn't hear the bell. Poor old Sid spent a freezing cold night, slumped spark-out on the doorstep, until he was found by the milkman. Blue, he was. Three days in hospital before they'd let him go. *Then* he got into trouble with his wife. Ruined his Christmas . . .'

Another frequent cause of accidents, apparently, is the angler relieving himself on the bank, as he has to in the absence of public conveniences, deep in the cover of the undergrowth. Nettle rash is common enough, but far worse are stings and bites from small insects.

'One bloke was bitten by a gnat,' said John, trundling on remorselessly. 'You wouldn't believe this, but by the time he got home, his willy was the size of a small marrow. A horrible purple colour, too. He didn't want to tell his wife what was wrong, but she insisted. Fat lot of help she was.'

'Why?'

'When he showed her his willy she fainted clean away.'

'Thanks, John. I'm trying to drink this pint, if you don't mind.'

'Oh, you've heard nothing yet. I could hear the screams of one poor lad a quarter of a mile away.'

'What had he done?'

'Just gone for a jimmy riddle in the undergrowth. What he didn't see was an electrified cattle fence. Wasn't a high voltage, thank God, but it certainly brought the tears to his eyes.'

'I bet it did. How was he afterwards?'

'You could say,' said John, snorting into his glass, 'that he was feeling a little dicky.'

Served me right for asking.

CHAPTER 10

A Collection of Characters

Mrs Layton died peacefully at the age of 91.

She survived the last eleven years on sheer courage and determination. She lived in a neat little bungalow with her bachelor son Dick who, as well as holding a responsible job on the council, did a bit of farming on the four-acre plot upon which their bungalow was sited. There was a half-acre apple orchard and a three-acre field in which Dick used to plant a yearly cereal crop.

This smallholding rated quite a number of agricultural implements and scattered about the place were old tractors, harrows, ploughs. I don't know what profit it brought Dick but it certainly gave him an interest and definitely a lot of hard work.

Mrs Layton was a lovely, quietly spoken, busy little lady who kept a spotless house and took tremendous care of Dick.

Dick was a very nice hardworking affable man who thought the world of his mother. As far as she was concerned, nothing was too much trouble; if there was anything she wanted, whatever it was, somehow Dick would produce it.

Mrs Layton hadn't been too well for a good number of years, but round about her 80th birthday her health began to deteriorate rather rapidly.

She had very severe arthritis, some heart trouble and skin trouble. We kept her going with various medications, she saw several specialists and still managed her home.

Dick's tea was always ready on time and Dick always took her breakfast in before he went off in the mornings.

Another very important member – and she could certainly call herself a member – of the household, was the auxiliary nurse. Lynne called in at least once a week, initially to help Mrs Layton with her bath, tend to her wants, perhaps do her hair and a whole variety of jobs, such as shopping, beyond the call of duty.

Nursing auxiliaries are very much unsung members of the National Health Service. They make such a difference, in very practical ways, to so many patients' lives. Lynne in particular had her own brand of cheerfulness and caring, not only with Mrs Layton, but with all the other people she visited. We depended on her as we did our district nurses and health visitors.

Although I routinely visited Mrs Layton, Lynne would always come and tell me if she thought she needed an extra visit. She really was a treasure.

Unfortunately, in spite of all the medication we gave her, Mrs Layton's health got progressively worse. Her main troubles were her hips. Her left hip, when I had it X-rayed, was fused solid, but her general condition was such that I couldn't risk sending her up for an operation. However, I was called to her in an emergency one day to find her lying in agony on the floor. She'd fallen and fractured her hip and had to go into hospital.

Her general health was so poor that I didn't think for a minute she could cope with an operation, but after she had been in hospital for a couple of weeks, with talk about traction, she was sent to theatre and given a total hip replacement.

She took longer than is usual to get over it, but in a month she was home, walking about better than she had been for a year or two.

Although each year she lost ground a little and had several other medical emergencies – some awful skin trouble and a couple of visits to hospital – she still maintained her home. There was, of course, always a reason for her to maintain her home: she had Dick to look after.

This was not an Oedipus-complex type of situation: they were both forthright, caring people, and Dick sought every practical aid that would help Mother.

Eventually it got so that she couldn't dress herself. Lynne had to get her up in the morning and put her to bed at night. But I'd still find her in the kitchen, peeling the potatoes, walking around with a frame, hardly ever complaining. 'We do our best, Doctor,' she'd say. And so it went on. The date of the hip operation to the time of her death was about nine years, and without Dick and Lynne to support her she certainly wouldn't have survived that time. Without Dick to look after, she wouldn't have wanted to survive that time.

Her end, when it came, was peaceful. She literally just couldn't put one foot in front of the other, couldn't be left at home. We got her into a little nursing home and she died there after a fortnight.

She was a wonderful, courageous lady and I can see her serious little face as I sit and write this. Dick would have an awful time managing without her, but he was a very active and able man, occupied with all sorts of things, so eventually he would come to terms with it. Lynne, who had got to know her so well over so many years, was heartbroken to see her go. If I'd been asked twelve years before Mrs Layton died how long I thought she might live, I would have given her about a year. But she had a reason for staying alive and was loved and cared for. I think these things are probably the strongest medicines there are for the treatment of any patient.

*   *   *

Alma Tranton was one of my favourites. She lived alone in a very nice house about three miles from the surgery. She had a tiny dog who used to yap around whenever I came near, and would never come near enough to let me stroke him.

Alma kept pretty well. She'd led a very adventurous life, a great figure in the Girl Guides, and as a young woman had done all sorts of things. She'd been camping and exploring, and had sailed to Australia with a group of Guides in a boat. A real character.

She came from an army family and was born after her father's death in action, as he had been born after *his* father's death in action. In the First World War she'd lost 34 close relatives—cousins, brothers, sisters and uncles.

She had her father's diary, his day-to-day account of his experiences in one of the Afghan campaigns towards the end of the 19th century. I was fascinated by them and tried to get them published for her, but they were all about what happened to him and he failed to mention exactly what was going on in the war, so many publishers were not interested.

His descriptions were marvellous. He was either in the advance guard or the rear guard of the column as they marched to Kabul. When they made camp he'd go off fishing, or hunting for birds with his gun, and a great deal of his writing was devoted to his hobbies.

The officers had regular weekly mail from England. They obviously ate and drank well, with a glass of port every evening. War seemed much more clear-cut in those days. They were fighting heathens who were thought of more as a sort of sub-species rather than fellow human beings.

For much of the way, the column went by train. There's an account of an incident when the train couldn't get up the hill, so they all got out and pushed. Then, outside Kabul, they all stopped for the day and had a gymkhana. Alma Tranton's father won the 100-yard dash. Once they'd packed up the things from the gymkhana they picked up their rifles and set off to war again.

. . . I came back from a weekend off duty to find that Miss Tranton had been sent into hospital by Jack Hart. When I called to see her I found that she had a fractured femur.

'How did you do this, Alma?' I asked.

'Oh,' she said, 'I was playing football with the dog and fell over.'

This was typically Alma. She took it all in her stride, had a new hip put in, came back and resumed the running of a household.

She had a good home help and an invaluable friend, a teacher called Anne, whom she'd known since she ran a Guide troop. Alma in her mid eighties and Anne, about retiring age, used to go off together on holidays, caravanning all over England. Then as Alma got a little more frail, they gave up the caravan. At 85, Alma stopped driving herself and had to rely on Anne. Eventually Anne retired from teaching and spent more and more time with Alma. She didn't come and live with her all the time but they used to take it in turns: sometimes Alma staying with Anne at Guildford, sometimes Anne staying with Alma at Tadchester.

Although she became progressively limited in her movements, Alma was full of life. She was still going strong at 88 and, although I'd strictly forbidden her to play any more football with the dog, she kept on going; partly because she was the sort of person who would have always kept on going. It was because of her army background, and because she had a friend who cared for her and would come and look after her, repaying some of the kindness that Alma had shown her when she was younger.

*   *   *

Alfred Scott had cancer of the lung. It meant his going into hospital to have one of his lungs removed. However, the condition was caught early enough; he could manage perfectly well on one lung and he made a good recovery.

Naturally, he worried whether he might get a reccurence but, as he ticked off the years, he became more and more reassured. During this time his wife Elizabeth, although holding down a full-time job, had taken care of him.

He'd become fit enough to go back to work after a couple of years and his X-rays, the clinic, and I myself – at last, after six years – managed to reassure him that the disease that had ailed him was now in the past.

In this sixth year his wife Elizabeth had a heart attack and a stroke. She was severely incapacitated, dangerously ill, and came out of hospital with little use of one leg, and no use of one arm. She also had what is known as nominal aphasia, which meant that she could understand everything that was said to her but was unable to reply. She'd get all the words wrong. She'd say something like, 'It's in the basket,' and keep on repeating it. She was patiently nursed by her husband, who gave up work to look after her.

With physiotherapy she improved to such an extent that she could walk around the room, get in and out of her wheelchair and her speech slowly and steadily improved. In fact Elizabeth Scott slowly and continually improved over five years.

Jack used to take her out in the car. He would take her

94

wheelchair down a ramp from the house. She could hoist herself into the car, she could walk with a stick about 50 yards, and she made more and more sense with her speech.

They never grumbled, were always a great pleasure to go and see, and they were always delighted to see me. Elizabeth often needed a bit of reassurance, sometimes no more than my taking her pulse, and then she'd feel happy again.

She had one bad period – she wasn't sleeping very well and was getting depressed – so I ordered some tablets for her. They were a mixture of sleeping tablets and tablets to help her with depression; my prescription was for two at night.

The next time I saw her she was very very much better, thanked me for the tablets and asked for some more.

On my next visit she looked a bit pained and Jack explained to me that the new bottle only said two at night.

'That's what I ordered in the beginning,' I said.

Elizabeth had been taking two of these tablets three times a day. I would never ever order that many for anybody. I managed to get hold of my original prescription and discovered that it was, in fact, a dispensing mistake. But, strangely, this large dose of drugs completely transformed Elizabeth. Whether it reduced the considerable irritation from her stroke I don't know, but this dose of drugs which would have kept me asleep all the time, kept her awake, feeling much better, much more alert and solved most of her problems.

Twelve years after Jack's operation and six years after Elizabeth's stroke, they were still going strong, still enjoying life, still going on trips and outings. Keeping going because they needed each other. They couldn't manage without each other, a brave, resourceful couple who were leading as full a life as most people in spite of Elizabeth's limitations.

*   *   *

Another of my favourites was Alfred Black. Mr Black in his late seventies developed maturity-onset diabetes; that is to say, he'd got a bit of sugar in his water and had to take tablets for it.

His wife, who was a couple of years older than him and who used sometimes to get a bit confused, also developed diabetes a few years later.

Hers was more difficult to control. She started having trouble with her feet, and eventually had to have some of her toes amputated.

But she got over that and we got both of their blood sugar levels under control. I used to see Alfred at all the flower shows and agricultural shows. He used to write up the prizewinners for the local papers.

Again they were both a pleasure to meet. Unfortunately, Mrs Black got progressively confused and didn't know who her husband was sometimes, but they jogged along. I would sometimes pick up Mr Black from the bus stop when he was using his bus tokens to get to Winchcombe to get shopping he couldn't get in Tadchester.

The Blacks celebrated their Diamond Wedding anniversary and gave me one of the largest pieces of cake I've ever had to

eat, just in the middle of one of my many attempts to get slimmer.

They lived happily on for another three years and then Mrs Black's health deteriorated. She had to go into hospital and she died.

Mr Black was much helped by a niece until he got back on his feet again. He missed his wife a great deal, but she'd been a tremendous physical effort to look after the last few years. He used to come along to the surgery to see me, and always had a joke and a laugh. Only rarely after his wife died did he ask me to go and see him, and then only when he had something like bronchitis, which kept him in bed.

I had another great big piece of cake on his 90th birthday. I still give him lifts when I see him waiting for the bus into Winchcombe. He always has a twinkle in his eye, I always pull his leg, and he goes happily marching on.

* * *

I often think how lucky we are as general practitioners to be able to enter people's homes, to have an inner view of their lives, to appreciate that duty, love, friendship and just being plain nice are the secret formulae for staying alive.

Mrs Layton and Dick, Alma and Anne, Jack and Elizabeth Scott, Alfred and Mrs Black were just some representatives of the very best of people it was my privilege to look after.

I certainly got as much from visiting them as they got from me. They'd all lived great life spans, defeating impossible situations, showing tremendous courage and I was proud not only to call them my patients, but to call them my friends. There was little doubt in my mind either, that I needed them rather more than they needed me.

CHAPTER 11

Stirling Quality

Miss Stirling was the matron of a hospital for mentally handicapped people which, like so many similar buildings had previously been a Poor Law Home. On the main road between Stowin and Winchcombe, it was looked after mainly by a psychiatrist from Winchcombe, but Jack Hart was the attendant GP, calling regularly to deal with the day-to-day medical problems of the residents. I was his second-in-command, going when I was on duty or if he was away on holiday.

A number of the patients in this hospital were very happy people. Mentally handicapped, they'd spent all their lives in institutional care. They were large, happy children who lived to great ages with insufficient insight to appreciate problems, and who looked forward to their holidays, treats and surprises. In some ways they were lucky.

There was also a ward for very handicapped children who'd spent their lives in crash helmets and boxing gloves to prevent them coming to harm. Unable to communicate, incontinent, having to be fed, they were pathetic sights. The nurses were very attached to them, however, and voluntary visitors used to come and make special efforts to communicate with them.

Overall, Wayside Hospital was one of the best, most efficient, happiest, spick and span medical institutions I've been to.

It was spick and span because the matron, Miss Stirling, was one of those people who had the drive to get everybody enthusiastic about their work. Rather than wait for painters to come from the local area or group hospital, for example, the nurses painted the walls of their own wards. They organised fêtes, jumble sales and sponsored walks to provide special treats and amenities for all the patients. The unions grumbled that people were being done out of jobs but, with the state of the National Health Service, things just didn't get done without voluntary effort. The standard of care and cleanliness and facilities of this hospital were absolutely superb, and all due to the driving force of the matron.

Miss Stirling was so good that she got promoted. Promotion meant leaving her beloved Wayside Hospital and being in charge – as a sort of supervisor with no authority – of three hospitals: Wayside, St. Luke's and Field Farm. It also meant that one of the most useful women I've ever met in the National Health Service was now made completely impotent – simply because she'd done so well.

Because of some national economy cuts it was decided to close down Field Farm and its 20 beds. Miss Stirling and one of the psychiatrists from Winchcombe asked if they could buy it from the National Health Service and run it privately. This would take a great load off the National Health Service, as the house – once an old country house – was in a deplorable condition.

The authorities eventually agreed to allow them to purchase the property but charged them the full market price. Once they'd bought it, they made them build elaborate fire escapes and fit every other safety precaution that one could dream of, all at great cost.

Miss Stirling invited the best of her staff from Wayside Hospital to join her in this private venture. It couldn't be a charity; she didn't want it as a charity.

Between them, about half a dozen people set to in this great house, painted and decorated it throughout, and put up interior dividing walls. When they moved in it was almost derelict with leaking lavatories, broken furniture and filthy kitchens. They refurnished it and changed the decaying country mansion into a house with the fittings and amenities of a first class hotel.

I was approached by Miss Stirling to be on an ethical monitoring committee. It wasn't necessary, according to the book, but she thought it would be nice to have a little committee to keep an objective eye on the establishment, and to be an alternative body for the residents to come to if they had any particular worries.

One of the staff Miss Stirling had brought over from Wayside Hospital was the cook, who was from now on classified as a trainer.

In fact there were no members of staff; they were all trainers. There were no patients; they were residents. There was no central dining room but three dining rooms with six or seven residents in each.

The man who wired up the building gave up his job and stayed on as a trainer. It was one of his responsibilities to supervise the residents who worked in the gardens. Field Farm hoped to grow most of its own vegetables and be as self-supporting as possible.

All the residents took part in the preparing of meals, the cleaning of the house, making the beds. It was home, and they all had to play some part in the running of it.

Although it was supposedly a private residential home, i.e. it wasn't under the National Health Service, all the residents were people whose only source of income was the Department of Health and Social Security, and they allowed Miss Stirling £133.00 per head per week.

Miss Stirling and the psychiatrist had had to mortgage their homes, produce every bit of money they had, and raise bank loans just to purchase the building. It was to be non-profit making.

Despite the dilapidated state the building was in before Miss Stirling took it over, the cost per resident per week allowed under the National Health Service had then been £330.00, almost three times what Miss Stirling was receiving now. But she managed.

She managed because she had the ability to get the best out of people and had assembled a group of dedicated workers. This, as far as I was concerned, was another face of private enterprise.

There must be a lesson to be learnt. We hear of how under-financed our National Health Service is, but Miss Stirling showed how the right person can run a more efficient unit at a third of the cost. You can bet that Field Farm, like any other National Health Service hospital I know, was crying out for money to have various things done before Miss Stirling took it over.

She was quite adamant that they were not a charity, they were part of the community. She made sure that the residents didn't go about in groups; although they were mentally handicapped, they used to go out in ones or twos, not always with an escort. They might go to a pub or cinema and they occasionally did go out *en masse* to something like a pantomime. They all had £5 a week pocket money and a post office savings book and were encouraged to fend for themselves. Field Farm wanted to give to the community at large, as well as accept from it, and the residents and staff went down and painted the local village hall.

The residents did sometimes cause problems. One of the men every week spent his £5 on cigarettes, which he smoked incessantly until they were finished. They tried every way they could think of to make him stop. Finally Miss Stirling suggested he might try hypnotism, and explained patiently that it would mean a man waving a finger in front of his face. The smoker thought about it for 48 hours, then announced his decision. 'No,' he said. 'Watching that finger might damage my eyes.'

The whole project was a tremendous effort by a few dedicated people and makes me wonder about the welfare state. Has it emasculated us? Although it was started with the best intentions of providing security for everybody, to some extent we've encouraged some people not to try and fend for themselves.

They've been brought up to believe that the state is responsible and takes care of everything, even aged relatives.

One rather bad example of this is given by two patients who arrived in the practice, to live in a council house. They paid no rent, they were given £400 to furnish the kitchen, £400 to furnish the lounge, most of which they spent on drink, and there was no supervision. They had two lodgers which they weren't supposed to have, and their days were spent begging and pinching from their neighbours. They would never try and find employment – they even managed to con £10 out of me when they first arrived. Thinking they were in trouble I asked the health visitor to go round and see if she could help them. She found that their income was in fact higher than her own salary.

Miss Stirling and Fair Farm provide a ray of hope in this disintegrating society we live in. It takes me back to the collective thoughts of three wise old men I knew many years back who said that it's not better systems we need, just better individuals – as we have with Miss Stirling and her group.

CHAPTER 12

Blessed are the Meek

Stephen Maxwell was the senior partner when I first arrived in the practice at Tadchester. I served my apprenticeship with him and I've always said he was a saint in disguise, one of the finest men I've ever met.

He worked desperately hard, coming in every Sunday and taking fewer holidays than we did. In his spring holiday fortnight, he put his potatoes in. In the autumn holiday fortnight, he dug his potatoes up.

When he'd come as a young man to the practice, there'd been the senior partner, a Doctor Watson, his very dominant wife who ran the practice, and their mentally-ill daughter.

Just before I arrived this whole ménage had moved out to the country where Steve virtually supported them. There's some complicated story that Steve promised Doctor Watson, and I never knew in what circumstances, that he would look after his wife and daughter, and that he would never marry while Doctor Watson was alive.

Steve stuck to his word and he actually married, at the age of 67, an ex-teacher called Nancy Doone, a member of one of the old Tadchester families.

He worked only part-time after his marriage for a couple of

months and then gave up work altogether. This was not just the demands of his marriage but the fact, he'd kept from us, that he was unwell. Though he hadn't looked well before his marriage, none of us knew that he'd been seeing a specialist and had various kidney and blood pressure troubles.

It seemed such a shame that he'd had to wait until he was 67 before he got married, but he was blissfully happy with his new wife. They had a nice house with a large greenhouse Up-the-Hill. Though I missed not seeing him in the surgery every day, it was great to be able to pop in and have a cup of tea with them, wander round his garden and admire his greenhouse. He kept us supplied with tomatoes, cucumbers and lettuce the whole summer.

*　　*　　*

We had to find a replacement partner for Steve, as his workload was so great. Rather than advertise in the *British Medical Journal* and have a hundred applicants, we passed the word around that we were looking for somebody and soon had five candidates recommended to us. The great problem was that each one of the five would have done us.

We finally settled on one very nice young man called David Lichen who, after doing his house jobs and vocational training, had spent two years in the Falkland Islands as a GP. There, amongst other things, he had successfully imported and planted 1,000 trees. He'd also taken to the islands a Japanese car with a special four-wheel drive that would drive over practically everything. He could claim that he was one of the few people – perhaps the only one – to have run over a fish while driving through a river. He had a picture of himself holding some large fish with tyremarks right across its middle.

He was a lovely young fellow, worked very hard and was a good physician; very much loved by the patients, which was not surprising, as nothing was too much trouble for him.

The only criticism we had of him was that he wouldn't clear off on his half day – he always had unfinished work to do. It was almost as if he had brought the spirit of Steve Maxwell with him.

It was so nice in the practice having two young people as good as Catherine Carlton, our half-partner, and David. Although we found it hard to believe, all the rest of us were getting a bit long in the tooth. These young partners were not only nice, but were extremely well informed, able gently to educate us in new techniques and advances in medicine.

*   *   *

All seemed to be going well with Steve and Nancy's marriage until one day we had an emergency call from a hospital in Yeovil. Steve and Nancy were on their way back from holiday when Steve had been taken ill with chest pains. He'd had a coronary thrombosis but the word from the hospital was that there was nothing too much to worry about.

I drove out to Yeovil on my half day and was reassured to see Steve sitting up brightly in bed, smiling as usual, and Nancy with him. All appeared to be well, thank God.

Steve was due to be discharged back home at the weekend. I was so pleased I'd gone to see him and was reassured that he looked so well.

Three days later Steve had a second coronary and died straightaway.

It took me a long, long time before I could really take it in. He was without doubt the nicest and kindest man and best doctor that I've ever met, and suddenly he was gone. He'd been married just twelve months. It all seemed so unfair.

His poor wife Nancy was devastated. Steve was her life. None of us had any idea how long they'd loved each other, but having at last been able to marry him, to lose him so soon was more than she could bear.

It was no coincidence that three or four months after Steve's death it was found that Nancy had cancer. Henry operated on her, but he came back from the operation with a gloomy face. 'I'm afraid,' he said, 'I've only been able to remove part of the tumour. The outlook's very poor.'

The news was broken to Nancy that the operation had only been partially successful. Instead of upsetting her, it seemed to make her more cheerful. She always seemed full of beans, either when we went to see her, or when she came to see us after her discharge from hospital.

Nancy was really just longing to die and be back with her Steve. She deteriorated very rapidly and was buried in the same grave as Steve within one year of his death. She died without any regrets about leaving life. She was just rejoining this beloved man, without whom life had no meaning.

The whole town mourned their passing. Steve had been in practice in Tadchester for more than 40 years and Nancy had spent all her life in the town.

All my partners were good men, good doctors and, what was more, good friends, but Steve was a man apart. I shall never forget him. You couldn't really describe him as being meek but he could be described as being blessed. The biblical phrase, 'Blessed are the meek for they shall inherit the earth,' was about the most fitting epitaph you could give to this finest of men.

107

CHAPTER 13

C. P. and the Horseless Carriage

My friend Chris Parfitt did not have the luck with cars. If any car was stranded, broken down by the side of the road around Tadchester, the local bookies would have laid reasonable odds that it belonged to C. P.

Basically it was lack of interest in the horseless carriage: C. P. reckoned life to be too full of more interesting objects and pursuits than motors and motoring. He could never have fallen in love with a car and spent the weekend polishing it, as did many of the Tadchester motoring enthusiasts. In fact he only had a car at all on condition that his wife Joyce looked after the cleaning of it.

He was not mechanically-minded. What went on under the bonnet was a complete mystery to him, and local garage proprietors made a steady living out of putting right for him what the average schoolboy could have fixed in a couple of minutes. Once he called out a mechanic because his car would not start from home. It took the mechanic all of ten seconds to diagnose a chronic lack of petrol, without which even the most finely-tuned engine has difficulty in turning over.

He could never tell one make of car from another. When asked what his new car was, he'd reply, 'A maroon one.' And mean it.

After he passed his driving test, his instructor congratulated him and asked, 'And how do you find driving in the Hillman Minx?'

'I don't know,' said C. P. 'I've never driven one.'

'Look at those letters on the wing of the car you've been learning in for the past twelve months,' said the instructor. 'What do they say?'

C. P. spelled them out. 'M-I-N-X,' he said. 'Well, would you credit it?'

After his first abortive call to the Automobile Association, he kept a card under the dashboard recording such details as Registration Number, Make of Car, Year of Manufacture . . . all the essential information which for the life of him he could never remember.

He was God's gift to the second-hand car salesman. He worked on a basis of trust. He told the salesman how much he could afford, and asked in return for a serviceable car: nothing high-powered, sophisticated or flashy, just something which would go from point A to point B without any trouble.

The salesman would sell him a car which would go from point A to point B, but omit to mention that it was in no fit state to get to point C. If George Washington himself had sold a car to C. P., he would have been tempted to slip in the odd white lie. Never give a sucker an even break, they say. Where cars were concerned, C. P. was the world's Number One Sucker.

His local garage changed hands. Instead of a proprietor who would sell him a car guaranteed not to fall apart for a week or two, he dealt with a proprietor who sold him a car which should have been pressed into a cube long ago.

'Look at this,' said C. P. when he called round at my house on his first trip in the new car. 'Not bad, eh?'

Certainly it didn't look bad. The bodywork was gleaming from the garage's pre-sale buffing-up.

I offered my congratulations on his shrewd eye for a bargain, and off he drove. There was a resounding metallic crash as the car moved away, and a complete exhaust system fell at my feet.

That particular car disgraced itself a few weeks later when

C. P. and his family drove up to Manchester for a niece's wedding, to be followed by a week's fishing on the River Lune at Lancaster. C. P. had heard from John Denton, the water bailiff, of a sure bait for salmon and sea trout: half a dozen lobworms threaded up the line like a snake. To make sure he had plenty of bait, he had packed several cans of prize lobworms from his compost heap, almost snake-sized themselves and lovingly cradled in moss.

As the car chugged up the M6 just south of Crewe, there was a horrible grinding sound from the engine. C. P. slewed on to the hard shoulder, where the car shuddered and stopped dead.

He opened the bonnet to be met by a cloud of oily black smoke. After administering the full range of his car repair techniques, which consisted of several minutes' colourful cursing and kicking hell out of the offside front wheel, he trudged off to an emergency phone and called the AA.

The patrolman diagnosed a seized-up engine, suggested that the AA Relay service be called to take the car back to its garage of origin, and that the family continue their journey by taxi.

The taximan arrived to find a weeping Joyce – upset by the possibility of missing the wedding – being comforted by her daughter Janet. Son Clive was climbing into the cab with the Relay truck driver, with instructions from his father to strangle the car salesman when the wreck was delivered back to Tadchester. C. P. himself, meanwhile, was the calm in the centre of the storm: sitting amidst a pile of luggage on the hard shoulder, gently sorting through his worms to make sure that the journey so far hadn't upset them.

'First things first,' he said. 'You can't get worms of this quality just anywhere.'

They made the wedding in Manchester just in time, then travelled up by train to Lancaster. Clive, who was a 20-year-old undergraduate was big enough and articulate enough to put the frighteners on the most villainous used-car salesman, had the engine fixed in double-quick time back in

Tadchester and drove up to join the rest of the family on the Lune.

The journey back – or half of it – was impressive. C. P. had a passion for auction sales and had a habit of bidding for the least desirable object. Joyce often had to restrain him from buying moth-eaten stuffed bears or mooses' heads that had seen better days.

At an auction in Lancaster, Joyce made the mistake of nipping out to the toilet. She returned in time to see the auctioneer knocking down a pair of buffalo horns. (Texas longhorns, really, but used as an object of veneration in the Royal Antedeluvian Order of Buffalo lodges throughout the British Isles.) This pair was enormous – six foot four from tip to tip, possibly the biggest pair known to man.

'My God,' she said to C. P. 'What idiot's bid for those things?'

'Sold,' said the auctioneer, 'to the gentleman in the glasses over there.'

Joyce looked around for the idiot in the glasses, then noticed the auctioneer's gavel pointing straight at C. P.

'What the –?'

'Ssh,' said C. P. 'I'll explain later. Always wanted a pair of those. A bargain, too. Only fifteen quid.'

The auctioneer moved on to the next lot, muttering under his breath, 'There's always *one* . . .'

C. P. soon solved the problem of transporting the horns back to Tadchester by strapping them on the roof rack of the car. He strapped them on crossways, as worn by their original owner, figuring that if he laid them on longways he'd run the risk of spearing somebody. Besides which they looked better that way.

The longhorned car made a spectacular progression on the way back to Tadchester, drawing what C. P. took to be admiring glances from other motorists. But just as the car was approaching the M5, it was overtaken and flagged down by a police patrol vehicle.

On the hard shoulder, C. P. wound down the window and smiled ingratiatingly at the large policeman.

'May I have your name, sir?' asked the patrolman.

'Certainly, officer. Parfitt. Chris Parfitt.'

'I see. I thought for a moment I'd got Buffalo Bill. Shoot it yourself, did you, sir?'

The penny dropped through the officer's heavy sarcasm, and Chris explained about the buffalo horns.

'Certainly a bargain,' said the patrolman. 'And very tasteful, I'm sure. But tied on like that they constitute a dangerous load. We don't want to have any motorcyclists stuck on the horns of a dilemma, do we sir? Now get them strapped on the other way!'

With some puffing and struggling from C. P., and some muscular and more expert help from Clive, the horns were finally arranged pointing back and front. Joyce tied a white handkerchief round the tip of each, just to make sure they would be seen.

'That's much better, sir,' said the officer. 'Safe journey. And the best of luck at the rodeo . . .'

'Smart-arse,' said C. P., *sotto voce*.

The next year's holiday saw the final demise of the old car. Or at least, the old engine. Again, the trouble started at an auction in Lancaster, where C. P. bought a huge art nouveau sideboard. It was a magnificent piece of furniture, or would be when it was cleaned and polished up, and again it was a bargain. But getting it home made the problem of the buffalo horns fade into nothing.

The cost of having it sent by road or rail would have been about ten times what C. P. had paid for the thing. So he decided to risk the roof rack. All the luggage was crammed into the boot and squashed in odd corners of the car's interior. The massive sideboard was lashed down firmly, and the family set off.

'Why do we always have to look like Ma and Pa Kettle?' asked Joyce.

There was no answer to that.

C. P. took the first driving shift and made sure he kept down to a reasonable speed. But halfway home, he and Clive swapped seats and C. P. settled down for a snooze. Clive was going back to university in a couple of days and he was eager to get home and pack . . .

When C. P. woke up, he was aware of a heavy labouring noise from the engine. He glanced across at the speedometer.

'Seventy? For God's sake, Clive! Not with that thing on top!'

'It's OK, Dad,' said Clive. 'It's a big engine. It'll take it.'

'Not for long, it won't!' yelled C. P. 'Pull in at the next service station and let's check that the sideboard's still strapped on all right.'

Clive pulled in at the next service station and C. P. got out. He was moving round the car, checking the lashings, when his foot slipped. Looking down, he saw a large patch of smoking oil spreading from under the car. He threw up the bonnet and checked the oil dipstick, one of the few things he knew the location of. There was about enough oil to lubricate a small watch.

It was a long and slow journey home. When the engine had cooled down, C. P. bought a large can of oil and used it to refill the engine. Then he bought another can for the journey, stopping every few miles to fill the car up again, and buying several more cans before they finally made it to Tadchester.

'A very nice piece of furniture,' I said to C. P. admiring the sideboard with its art nouveau decorations, both in carved relief and in different coloured veneers, which weeks of Joyce's elbow grease had revealed. 'Would you mind me asking how much you paid for it?'

'Not at all,' said C. P. 'Twelve quid, that was.'

'You got a real bargain there.'

'I certainly did. Twelve quid. Oh . . . and £600 for a new engine. Still, it could be worse.'

'Worse?'

'A lot worse. I could do it for a living . . .'

CHAPTER 14

Winter Break

We were having a cold and miserable winter; there just seemed no end to it. In Tadchester we were either ploughing through snowdrifts or being lashed by freezing rain.

On impulse, Pam and I booked a holiday only two weeks before the departure date to somewhere we knew we couldn't be guaranteed sunshine, but where the weather should be better than we were having at home.

We'd chosen the town of Faro in the Algarve in Portugal, known mainly for its airport. Everybody going to the Algarve has to land there and pick up their coach or hire car to one of the many resorts: Portugal's resorts are increasing almost at the rate of the Spanish resorts in the Sixties.

Nobody seems to stay in Faro. Everybody we questioned, even people who had time-share villas in the Algarve and landed at Faro two or three times a year, had never visited the town.

What we didn't want was a recurrence of what happened on a holiday after my coronary bypass operation three years previously.

We had landed in a concrete jungle in the south of Las Palmas in the Canary Islands, where there was no indigenous population, just endless rows of hotels and apartments, and supermarkets that all sold the same stuff.

There was only one hotel in Faro in the brochures and this was the Hotel Eva, with 150 bedrooms, overlooking the harbour. We booked a room with a sea view and a bathroom. I reasoned, if the worst came to the worst, I could sit in the bath looking out over the harbour. Although we were on bed and breakfast terms, these also included afternoon tea – what Englishman could resist that?

We read up as much as we could about Faro and it did seem an interesting little town. The first book ever printed in Portugal was printed in Faro in about the 15th century. As a budding author, I took this as a happy omen; perhaps it would give me just the atmosphere to do a bit of writing. Apparently the town was spoilt in the 16th century by the beastly English, who knocked the place down on Queen Elizabeth's orders. Subsequently a couple of earthquakes in the 18th century had done the place no good at all. Following these, a very energetic bishop had made everybody do the Portuguese equivalent of 'pull their fingers out' and got a thriving port going again, with marble works and salt works. Today even – not the bishop's doing – there are light industry and plastics. There were also promises of shopping precincts, plenty of restaurants, shopping arcades: it all sounded very nice. What sounded nicest of all was that it would probably be filled with Portuguese, who are our oldest allies and some of the nicest people on earth. (We'd had two holidays in Madeira which we loved, and I think there's nobody better than the Portuguese for looking after you: they are courteous, kind, smiling lovable people.)

Setting off in midwinter had its complications – the partners didn't look too pleased, the workload was heavy. But we were only going for a week and some of the others had been off skiing. At home, we had Bertie to think of and worries about frozen pipes and other such nasties which were epidemic at that time.

The day was saved by our Norman, who offered to come and live in the house and look after Bertie, whom he'd known since a puppy.

Our Norman first came into our lives when I was put off work with chest pains, just before my coronary bypass. I was unable to do much physical work at the time and we needed some help in the garden. Word got round that Norman might be able to spare us a day and he called to interview us. A brisk, cheery, smiling man who said: 'I'm very happy to come and help you. My name's Norman, you're Pam, you're Bob, and the first time I hear myself called "the bloody gardener", I'm off.'

Norman was a phenomenon. Although he was past retiring age, I would match him against any 25-year-old for the sheer physical graft he could put in one day's work.

When we first met him he was working two days a week, for virtually nothing, to help out at a home for mentally handicapped children. He then had ourselves and two other customers, who only rewarded him a little more.

None of his earnings was essential, he could have lived without them, but what he couldn't do without was his travelling.

Every year for one month he used to take his car and go camping in France. He'd done this for ten years since losing his wife. He knew more about France than any other man I'd met. But France was only the main holiday.

Over the three years we'd known him he'd also had holidays in Tunisia, Sorrento, Rouen, Athens, Morocco, splitting up his time between Marakkesh and Agadir, then a separate holiday in Tangier and another one in Lisbon. Before we met him he'd been to Australia, and Germany – East and West. You name it, Norman had been there.

A six-year spell of army service during the war had given him his taste for travelling. He had arrived in France just as most of the other troops were leaving at Dunkirk. Norman's French campaign was short: he drove 60 miles from Cherbourg, 60 miles back and returned to England. Then, after the invasion of North Africa, he was stationed for three years in Algiers.

Gardening had always been a great hobby of Norman's and he'd many a time won Best Gardener competitions as a young man. He had been a printer by trade and having been 30 years in the business, then worked for an industrial firm. At retirement age, he didn't retire: he just moved in another direction and worked five or six days a week from eight in the morning till four in the afternoon.

During his working life, it wasn't enough for Norman just to have a full-time job during the day. At night he had his own dance band which played for organisations like Round Table and Rotary, as well as for civic functions. He still retained his love for music and just occasionally we could coax him to play us something on the piano.

Norman came to us every Wednesday and became part of the family. He was a meticulous, well organised man. He arrived not at 7.59 in the morning, nor at 8.01. On the dot of eight o'clock, up the drive would come Norman's car. At three minutes past eight either the lawnmowers would be whirring or you'd see Norman with a barrow already filled with soil pushing it up to some corner of the garden.

I'm very sloppy about most gardening jobs, but Norman soon put me right. When, after my operation I was fit enough to do some gardening myself, he would fairly jump on me if I was putting up a fence or something and didn't do it properly.

Out would come Norman's ruler: if a job had to be done it had to be done properly and precisely. He was a craftsman, a man who kept up all the old standards, and he completely transformed our garden.

He would occasionally stay for a meal, or sometimes we would take him out for a meal. He was good company, great fun to be with, and much appreciated good food and wine. He had become, since living on his own, a most skilled and discriminating cook.

His house was an absolute joy, beautifully furnished and decorated. We were very lucky to be associated with him and had the greatest respect for him and for his judgement. A quite remarkable man.

It was a great comfort, leaving the house in the winter, to know that Norman would be there. Bertie loved him and every Wednesday he'd go absolutely mad with joy as soon as he heard Norman's car approaching.

We settled Norman in. I left some wine on my wine rack and said if it wasn't drunk by the time we came back, it wouldn't be Norman giving *us* the sack – he would be dismissed on the spot.

Norman lived quite close, so Bertie could go back and forth with him to home and we could set off without worrying about anything. Eventually, set off we did.

Fortunately we caught an early train to London, setting off the day before our flight was due and spending a night in a hotel near Heathrow, to be sure we'd be there for take-off. It was as well we did: the train journey to London, instead of taking the usual four to five hours, with changes, took nine. The countryside was covered in snow, and there were delays caused by frozen points and huge shifting snowdrifts.

*   *   *

Our flight from Heathrow to Faro passed quickly, not just because we had a meal served in the middle of it, but because I unintentionally eavesdropped on a conversation in the row behind me.

A Portuguese gentleman in a fashionably washed denim suit, with dark glasses and high black boots – he looked like the local Mafia representative – was chatting up an English lady, who didn't seem to be averse to his approaches. I learned all about their families, their cars, their hopes, their ambitions, their invitations, their telephone numbers; even the time they were going to meet in Lisbon. 'Another drink to our friendship, Belinda,' said the Portuguese gentleman as the umpteenth round arrived.

When we eventually arrived at Faro, however, and it came to luggage-carrying time, he scuttled off to look after his own stuff and Belinda was left to cope with her own. She was very good looking, but she appeared a very sensible lady too, not likely to be swayed by a few drinks and a bit of smooth talk. Somehow I didn't think they'd make it as a pair.

The Hotel Eva looked exactly like it did in the brochure, which was a very pleasant surprise. We had a nice double room

119

and a balcony overlooking the harbour which was filled with small boats.

What I hadn't realised was how much the Algarve had been waiting for us to arrive. A girl in traditional dress had thrust a flower into Pam's hand as we left the airport. There was a card attached to it saying that this entitled us to 3,500 escudos, about £2, if we'd go and have a look at the Four Seasons Country Club. In our room was a letter and a picture from Henry Cooper, God bless him, who was offering me a complimentary golf lesson, a complimentary round of golf and a cheque for £10 for the Variety Club Sunshine Coach appeal fund, if only I would have a look at the luxury apartments and golf course at Penina.

And this was just the beginning. There was a letter from a lady called Trish, who apparently had a desk somewhere in the hotel. If we would go and spend a day at the exciting new holiday resort of Portobello, we'd have a free lunch, a bottle of wine and could win one of several marvellous prizes of free holidays, free meals or money. Stamped across it was the legend: 'Married couples only. One gift per family or group. If married, must be accompanied by spouse.' Obviously, they were having no hanky panky.

Acting on my principle that there's no such thing as a free meal, I slipped all the invitations quietly into the wastepaper basket.

We awoke on our first morning to glorious sunshine. We had breakfast served in our room and sat eating it on the balcony. Overhead was a clear blue sky; down below was a picturesque harbour full of bobbing boats. Back home, Britain lay shivering under a blanket of freezing snow. Was all this real?

Faro is a lovely little town, and it *is* a town, not a hideous concrete resort. And I believe it has more fire engines per head of population than any other town I've been to.

Just a few yards down from the official fire station which had a whole line of fire engines, most of them vintage enough to claim a place in the London-to-Brighton race, was another fire station with bold letters over the top, proclaiming: '*Bombeiros*

Voluntarios'. This was the volunteer fire brigade, equipped with a further dozen appliances, none of which looked as if its engine could be coaxed into life.

There was no doubt that firefighting was a big thing in Faro and that afternoon, a Sunday, we had a splendid display from the Bombeiros Voluntarios. There was some sort of swearing-in ceremony then a whole band of volunteer firemen – drums, bugles and red berets – set off to parade around town.

It was the first band I'd seen that had a real drum major. In England, drum majors are men who are basically non-commissioned officers who walk in front of bands, dressed up to the nines and swinging a great stick.

The Bombeiros Voluntarios' drum major was the man with the biggest drum in the band, who led the band and banged away louder than any. That for me is a real drum major – the man with the major drum.

If it should ever be my lot to live in Faro there is no doubt that I shall certainly join the Bombeiros Voluntarios. Perhaps one day I'd make it to drum major.

Our hotel was extremely comfortable and I found that it had all the polite hospitality that I associate with the Portuguese. Nothing was too much trouble, everything was relaxed. The dining room was a bit of a disappointment, though the staff were courteous and what the food lacked in quality, it made up for in quantity.

Happily, on the ground floor there was what was called a snack bar which was actually a first-class, very inexpensive restaurant where you could get any sort of meal from nine in the morning until eleven at night. It was spotless, the food was excellent and a good meal could be had for £4 or £5, with snacks for much less.

There was a free guided walk around town led by the room manager of the hotel, a lovely plump man with a great sense of humour.

We saw three fascinating museums. The Maritime Museum was beautifully laid out, with splendid models of early sailing ships. The Archaeological Museum in an old convent had some beautiful Roman mosaics which had been dug up in the town. The Ethnographic Museum showed the traditional ways of life in the Algarve, with photographs, paintings and everyday objects. Both the Ethnographic and the Maritime Museums had models of the complicated net structures used for catching tuna fish.

Pam and I are not great people for churches and historic places, but the museums and churches of Faro were special – tremendous care had been taken in setting everything up – so they were both interesting and entertaining.

The town itself was big enough to wander round. There were lots of little side streets, and we were so lucky, at least for the first day-and-a-half when the sun shone. There was a large pedestrian shopping precinct, first-class shops, innumerable shoe shops, plenty of restaurants and snack bars. I had my shoes cleaned for £1 – and noticed that the locals were charged 50p.

I wanted to get a mental picture of the whole of the Algarve, so we took a coach trip from Faro to Sagres. The day we set off on our coach tour was one of the wettest, windiest days I've ever experienced. We visited Albufeira. The last time I'd been there, 17 years ago, it was a nice little resort with a few hotels. Now it was a concrete jungle, similar to the ones I'd seen in Las Palmas. It looked frightful, but I expect if you are 20 and all you want is sun, sea, bars and music in the summer it's just the place to go. It certainly looked pretty grim on this wet and windy day.

Portimão, a fishing port we passed through, didn't seem to have changed much in the 17 years; fishing vessels were still coming up and unloading their sardines on the quay. Then lunch at Lagos, the principal maritime base of Prince Henry the Navigator, one of Portugal's great heroes, celebrated by a large statue on the waterfront. We forgot that the Portuguese sailors going off to explore new continents had much less knowledge of what they were going into than our astronauts going out into space today.

We passed on through Sagres, visiting Prince Henry's Fort,

finally arriving at Cape St. Vincent which people used to think was the end of the world. I can easily see how this happened: if it wasn't the end of the world, it should have been. It was the wettest windiest place I've ever known, with a gale blowing of frightening velocity.

I'd heard the expression, 'Lean against the wind', but this was ridiculous. Two of our lady passengers were blown completely off their feet, and you could only stand up if you were actually holding on to something. I had brought an umbrella which lasted two minutes in this torrential gale of rain and wind. For all that, it was a magnificent sight with the waves smashing themselves against the rocks.

On the way back the roads were blocked twice by fallen trees.

When I asked our guide if the weather was often like this, she said, 'No. The last time was 1946.'

That day happened to be the 600th anniversary of Britain and Portugal becoming allies. Prince Charles and Princess Diana, I saw later on television, were in Lisbon, and having just about as rough a time as we were.

But it was all fun, it was all adventure. We had made friends with a Canadian couple from Vancouver, Connie and Lloyd Measner, whose life story was a book itself.

Lloyd had been working on a prairie farm between the wars during the great depression when the great cereal plains became a dust bowl. He and Connie had met in the Yukon, working in the old goldfields. I tried to encourage him to write his memoirs – he had a fascinating story to tell – and I hope by now it's well under way.

What we liked about the hotel, apart from the care and consideration of the staff, was that there was always something going on. Every night there was music of some sort, and one night we had an excellent exhibition of Portuguese dancing, far better than anything I'd seen in Madeira. This was the real thing.

We were dragged out on the floor to join in the last two dances and, once on the floor, had to take part in a dance competition for residents, in which I am proud to say we came third. I left the floor with a bottle of wine, a gramophone record which I am sure is about time-share apartments, and a badly wrenched sternum, which had already suffered enough by being sawn in two during my coronary bypass operation. The wrenched sternum was my own fault: thinking I was a young man again, I picked up Pam in the rock 'n 'roll session and started to throw her about as I did 30 years ago.

There's always something happening in a town as opposed to a resort – a town has always to go on living. Faro is a lovely little town. You could catch a bus to the beach about eight kilometres away, and with Connie and Lloyd we caught the local train to the fishing port of Olhão. This is a real port, a real working town with a bonus of excellent shops and huge markets of both vegetables and fish.

We watched the sardine boats unloading and this was real graft – the fish were literally coming in by the ton. In addition, the small power boats were coming off the mud flats with huge net bags, probably weighing a hundred weight each, containing what looked very much like cockles. You really felt you were in the heart of Portugal.

The harbour at Olhão was surrounded by factories, and there was every chance that my Sunday night sardines on toast came from there.

I loved the laid-back attitude of the Portuguese. There were no bridges over the railway, you just wandered across the track. But at least the trains came exactly on time. On the way back we found we'd got into a first-class compartment by mistake. This meant we each had to pay an extra 30 pence. I only wish British Rail would copy their timetable and their fares.

Our week went only too quickly. There wasn't time enough to explore the town fully and there were many places locally that we would have liked to have visited, particularly the mountains. The day we set off to go back, of course, after the storms, it was blistering sunshine. But never mind: we'd had a great time and I was sure that Faro and the Hotel Eva would be seeing us again.

CHAPTER 15

Practice Makes Perfect

In spite of only a very small increase in the number of patients and a large increase in the size of our staff, life at the surgery became steadily busier and busier. Most of this was because we now offered a much more comprehensive service.

Our two practice nurses, Gill and Debbie, ran an open blood pressure clinic where you could always pop in and have your blood pressure taken. They also did all the dressings, ran a sort of weight-watchers clinic, did allergy testing and desensitisation. They did E.C.G.s for us and were gradually taking over quite a lot of the stitching up of cuts.

When I went to do a cervical smear I didn't have to wait while the woman got undressed behind the curtain in my room, I would be buzzed through by either Debbie or Gill to their treatment room and the patient would be already prepared for me. It was no longer just a case of a cervical smear, either: it was a well-woman clinic where a whole range of checks would be done.

It meant that we were practising a much better and higher standard of medicine, and patients were getting a much more comprehensive service.

I did, though, sometimes wonder whether we were getting

too mechanically minded. The dispensary seemed to grow another computer each day.

We had a special answering machine when we were on duty, in line with the computers, all of which frightened me to death. This answering machine would tell patients which doctor to ring after surgery hours.

It was quite simple before this new machine came. You just turned a switch, recorded a message, turned the switch back and there was the message. Now we had to turn about a dozen knobs, there was a great box with little red arrows, green bleeps, red bleeps. It was as though they'd put traffic lights on Birmingham's Spaghetti Junction.

You knew that it was set when a red light finally came on with an ear-splitting whistle. I really chuckled to myself one day when all our equipment failed; something to do with voltage levels. When the Electricity Board allowed voltage levels to fall below a certain level none of our equipment worked. Fortunately it only happened once, but it did show how vulnerable we were.

I was always being badgered to put my patients on the computer for their repeat prescriptions rather than see the patient myself and write the prescription on the spot. It was explained to me how much quicker and how much easier it was, but I'd never thought that ease and quickness were the main objectives of general practice. I'd always thought of us more as professional comforters who kept one eye open for people being ill, rather than just careful pill dispensers.

However, the other partners loved these new mechanical toys.

The pattern of surgery life changed as well. When I first started in practice, evening surgery began at six and went on until it finished, about half past eight or nine, but we didn't do so many of them. Now evening surgery started at four and finished at six. If the building wasn't cleared by 6.30, there was mass hysteria amongst our splendid staff.

In trying to work office hours, I think that we created many more pressures than when we took things more leisurely. Now, apart from the occasional home confinement, midwifery had disappeared into hospitals and our surgeries finished at six, but somehow we seemed to be busier and under greater stress. I think much of this was caused by trying to work to rigid time schedules.

You almost had one eye on the clock, thinking, 'Well I've got to finish this job or this visit, to be back at the surgery at such-and-such a time.' This tight schedule meant that a lot of our routine visiting, and I still did a lot (although this had again become unfashionable), had to be done after the evening surgery.

Some patients who'd been on medication for years, once they were told they were going on the computer for their medication, immediately gave up what they'd been taking. They didn't want to be treated by a machine. So although the computers were beneficial from the doctors' point of view, they were not everybody's cup of tea.

Everything is getting more efficient and more streamlined and I think this is one of the reasons why so many patients are turning from conventional medicine to alternative medicine.

I've always thought of medicine as an art. I don't think too many art students would be helped by computers.

I think the most important part of general practice is the communication between the patient and the doctor and the introduction of super efficient machinery does tend to come between them.

But I found myself in the same position as King Canute – I couldn't make the tide go back.

The surgery that I enjoyed the most was a little branch surgery in a village where there was no transport. I had to let myself in through a little side room off the church hall. There was a fire in the waiting room for the patients.

It was meant to service just the people in this small community. I would see them, make out the prescriptions, take the prescriptions back to the main surgery and have them made up. Later in the day I'd drop them down at Jones' Brothers, the paper shop in the village, and patients would collect them from there.

This surgery was like little Alice – it grew and it grew and it grew, until often it was my biggest surgery of the week. I would sometimes arrive there on a Tuesday morning to find people who couldn't fit in the waiting room standing outside the door.

It was very difficult to do a proper examination there and if it was anything really personal the patient had to come up to the main surgery at a later date.

As patients came in to see me I'd hear laughter and conversation from the main waiting room in the hall. It was like a village club. Something to be looked forward to each week. Meet all your friends, swap local gossip.

Eventually I had more patients coming from miles outside the village than I had villagers. This wasn't because I had any particular magic or was more popular than my partners, it was the fact that nobody had to make an appointment – everybody knew there was a surgery going on there and they knew all they had to do was to turn up.

I seemed to form a special relationship with the people that lived in this village.

I thought I might have to cancel my last surgery in the village before I retired from practice. I had to attend a coroner's inquest with a colleague in the morning. But I couldn't miss it. So I decided that instead of having it at eleven o'clock I'd have it at two o'clock. I put a message up on the church hall door 'Surgery changed to two o'clock'.

When I arrived at the church hall at two, there didn't seem to be many people about, certainly no cars outside. I let myself into my little consulting room and sat down. There was a knock on the door and in came Joyce Wallace, one of the stalwarts of the community.

It was a community that looked after itself, and Joyce was always to be found if somebody wasn't well or needed a meal or somebody needed running to hospital. The village ran its own aid service, getting people to and from hospital, either for medical treatment or for visiting friends and relatives.

'Oh, Doctor Bob,' said Joyce. 'Could you come in the waiting room a second?'

What was this? A casualty?

Joyce opened the door and there was the waiting room of the church hall absolutely packed with just about every villager, all on their feet clapping. I was completely taken aback.

'We all felt that we couldn't let you go away without showing our appreciation,' said Joyce. And there in the hall was a lovely garden seat and a great wrought iron flower bowl packed with geraniums and ferns – a beautiful sight, flowers of all colours tumbling over the side like a waterfall. I could have wept. I was going to miss this surgery the most of all.

There's a moral in it somewhere. They say that big is beautiful, but I've often found that small isn't so bad either.

*   *   *

Coupled with all these changes in the practice was a dearth of the old characters. Many of the old characters, of course, by definition, grew older and passed on, so that people like the cobbler, the blacksmith, the village grocer, the carpenter and the odd job man, disappeared. The old characters one could sit and yarn with and have a cup of tea with didn't seem to be there anymore. There were some exceptions, like our Norman, and Reg and Pam Dawkins. Reg led a successful and cheerful life from a wheelchair, and he and his wife produced the most potent home-made wine I ever drank. But even on the farms, where everything was becoming so scientific, people hardly had time to sit down for a drink and a chat.

However, like everything else, the whole circle was turning.

Young people were beginning to set up craft communities, hand-made furniture was available, and special jumpers from local wool. There were two or three new potteries. Individuals were wanting to do their own thing in their own way. People were determined not to become one of the mass but to express themselves freely, even though economically this might not be the most efficient way.

So I could foresee in the future a new generation of characters. It was strange to find, after more than 30 years in general practice, that the rugged individualists and interesting people were not now the 75-year-olds, but the 35-year-olds.

There were Alan and Edgar who could make the most beautiful hand-painted plates. Pam and I have the only one they made to celebrate the bringing up of the *Mary Rose*, a beautiful plate with the ship in the middle and a replica of Tudor design round the outside. In years to come, the plate will be a real treasure in its own right. Edgar's wife, Doreen, sculptured, painted, kept chickens, geese, and a donkey that kept all her neighbours awake with its braying.

Albert Coldheart, a patient and meticulous man, made the most beautiful models. I've had several from him including a pipe of peace and a French haycart. One Christmas, knowing of my interest in rivers and waterways, he made the most beautiful barge, accurate in every detail – lifting hatches, a walkway across, colourful, with the trading name of Robert Clifford and Company on it.

When I retired, Alan Caiger-Smith made me the most beautiful plate of a pheasant, wearing a stethoscope and

hanging up its boots. (One of my writing pseudonyms was Dr Pheasant.)

Another young patient, Jerry Walker, made the most beautiful 30-foot steam launch. He'd made every little bit of it himself, over six years. It was beautiful, mahogany with a cabin with glass engraved windows. Even the glass engraving he'd done himself, having gone to night school to learn how to do it. There were wicker-work seats to sit on; again he'd made them after lessons in the art at evening class.

One afternoon Jerry took Pam and me for a long trip on the boat down to the mouth of the estuary and back up, through Tadchester bridge, as far as the river was navigable. It was marvellous, pottering along, with the steam engine making hardly any noise at all. I could see how people loved steam.

All these characters and craftsmen were in their mid-thirties. And I think they, and people like them, might hold the answer to many of society's problems.

Machines are taking over from men in all the manufacturing industries and men are going back to the old cottage craft industries.

I can foresee a time when these things will equate, when the unpleasant difficult tasks will be done by machines and our furniture, crockery, pottery, fabrics, clothes will be, more and more, made by cottage-type industries.

With more time our leisure industries should grow, facilities should improve. What we have to do is learn how to use our leisure.

One of the wisest men that I've ever met put forward a proposition that nobody ever completely took up. His idea was that there should be no unemployment, that everybody who had not got a job should be put on the labour reserve and, to draw money for what had previously been called the dole, they would have to earn it. They would either have to learn a language, learn bricklaying, carpentry, to play a musical instrument or take part in the renovation of some of the amenities on, say, the canals and rivers. A scheme like this would increase men's skills, take away boredom and, above all, mean that men that have been pushed out by machines would be able to maintain their dignity and learn new skills. Already some steps are being taken in this direction but, with today's massive unemployment, obviously more are needed.

I remember the old Head of the London School of Economics in a television broadcast saying that society has to make up its mind whether to pay men to work or pay them not to work.

It does seem over the last few years that people have been paid, and not very well, for not working. How much better for everybody if this could be switched to the other alternative.

CHAPTER 16

Big Brother is Watching

A change took place in general practice, the most profound change that had occurred during the whole of my medical working life: probably even more profound than the actual nationalisation of medicine.

Government-inspired, it was the limitation of prescribing by doctors.

A list of drugs was issued, and general practitioners were limited to prescribing only the drugs on the list. In addition, and this addition was probably a sensible one, only the prescribing of generic names for drugs would be accepted. For example, if you prescribed Panadol tablets (a proprietary name instead of Paracetamol which is the same but much cheaper) your prescription was disallowed and you, as the doctor, had to foot the bill.

Although we had a reasonable choice, this meant we were no longer able to prescribe precisely.

After 30 years of medicine I had to change the whole of my prescribing habits. For example, instead of there perhaps being 20 different indigestion tablets, I was now limited to about two, and this pattern went through most of the drugs that we prescribed. There was, thankfully, no limitation on life-saving drugs.

The medical profession seemed to take it without too much fuss, but I don't think any of us appreciated how our freedom was being curtailed.

Gradually I adjusted to it. We were a dispensing practice and our dispensers were very good. They pointed it out if we strayed from the list or forgot to prescribe the generic formula of a preparation rather than its trade name. All seemed to go along smoothly. Too smoothly, perhaps: we had lost a precious freedom.

One January morning, I received a long letter which read as follows:

Dear Doctor Clifford,
Selective List Prescribing and Dispensing
It has been noted that during July 1986 you prescribed and dispensed items on Form FP.10 which are no longer permissible under the Regulations. Copies of the prescriptions were sent to you by the Prescription Pricing Authority and you were informed that payment for the items had been disallowed. The relevant paragraphs of your Terms of Service read as follows:

'36A – (1) In the course of treating a patient to whom he is providing treatment under these terms of service, a doctor shall not order on a prescription form a drug or other substance specified in Schedule 3A to these regulations but may otherwise prescribe such a drug or other substance for that patient in the course of that treatment.

(2) In the course of treating such a patient a doctor shall not order on a prescription form a drug specified in an entry in column 1 of Schedule 3B to the regulations unless –

    a) that patient is a person mentioned in column 2 of that entry.

    b) that drug is prescribed for that patient only for the treatment of the condition specified in column 3 of that entry; and

    c) the doctor endorses the face of that form with the reference "S3B".

but may otherwise prescribe such a drug for that patient in the course of that treatment.

38 – In the case of a doctor who is authorised or required by the Committee to supply drugs and appliances under regulation 30 to a patient, in the course of treating that patient under these terms of service that doctor –

    a) subject to paragraph 36A, shall record an order for supply under sub-paragraph (b), on a prescription form completed in accordance with paragraph 36(2), of any drugs and chemical reagents or appliances which are needed for the treatment of that patient, but, subject to regulation 30(10), shall not be required to issue that form to that patient.

    b) subject to regulation 30(10), shall supply for that patient under pharmaceutical services, where necessary in a suitable container, those drugs and chemical reagents or appliances but –

    i) shall not supply under those services for that patient any Scheduled drug, except that, where he has ordered a drug by a non-proprietary name, he may supply a drug which has the same specification notwithstanding that it is a Scheduled drug.

    ii) shall supply for that patient a drug specified in Schedule 38 to the regulations only where the conditions in paragraph 36A(2) are satisfied.

    c) may supply for that patient in respect of that treatment otherwise than under pharmaceutical services, any Scheduled drug, and may demand or accept a fee or other remuneration in respect of that supply.'

You will recall that on 11th June 1986 a letter was sent to you drawing attention to the change in the Regulations and pointing out that, having allowed a reasonable period for adjustment, the committee would in future have to consider taking formal action in those cases where breaches of the regulations occurred.

The subject was considered by a Special Reference Sub-Committee of the F.P.C. which has decided that, if infringement of the Regulations continues following receipt of this letter, they will have no option but to refer the matter to the Medical Service Committee. I must emphasise that this would undoubtedly result in a formal hearing before the Service Committee at which you could be found in breach of your Terms of Service. The Committee is anxious to avoid such an outcome if at all possible and therefore you are most strongly advised to exercise all possible care in the prescriptions which you sign and dispense.

It is hoped that you will accept this letter as the minimum action which can be taken at present and understand that the Committee is obliged to implement the statutory regulations.

Yours sincerely,

For Administrator

I just couldn't believe my eyes when I saw this letter.

I wrote a stinging reply back to the F.P.C. The F.P.C. is the Family Practitioner Committee, the country being split up into areas covered by various Family Practitioner Committees. The F.P.C. pay us, pay us for our drugs, and are usually extremely nice, helpful people.

My reply to this horrendous document started:

'When I received the enclosed letter, my first thoughts were that George Orwell was still alive and writing under a pseudonym for the Family Practitioner Committee. Please could you send me evidence of the heinous crime that I committed in July last year. (It was January when I received this letter.)'

I continued:

'We are now just one step away from my receiving a letter stating, "It has been reported that for three mornings running you were ten minutes late for your surgery, irrespective of the fact that you might have been up all night. Unless you can

provide some good reason for your lateness you will be up before the Medical Services Committee and have your bottom smacked."'

I then went on:

'We seem to have actually reached that stage. The caretaker of our surgery, a lovely old chap named Jack Richards, was reported by a nameless, faceless person for leaving work early. The fact that he arrived at work early and did a great number more hours than was required of him, and was an excellent workman, did not prevent him being suspended for about a month while the matter was being investigated. This brilliant piece of administration meant that we had to manage without a caretaker for a month.'

I concluded my letter by saying that general practitioners are a highly skilled, dedicated group of men who have tremendous workloads which include many unsocial hours, nights and weekend work, none of it compensated for by comparative time off. To be bothered on these lines borders on impertinence.

I then sent copies of our correspondence all over the place – local and national newspapers, my MP – and waited for evidence of the crimes I'd allegedly committed the previous July.

Each month I was writing on average about 1,300 prescriptions, so I should expect to make a few mistakes.

The Family Practitioner Committee produced only one prescription for an antihistamine which is not allowed – that was my only sin. But it wasn't even my sin; I hadn't signed or written the prescription. It was one of our junior partners but it happened to have my number on it.

I hit the roof. I rang John Bowler, my consultant physician friend, and asked whether there were any similar problems occurring in hospital practice.

'Oh, yes,' said John, cheerfully. 'We've just been told that in future they're going to stop calling patients patients, and call them customers. Presumably we're going to have an in-customer department and an out-customer department. At the least it should help bring the unemployment figures down.'

I asked my F.P.C. for the rise in the number of people that they'd employed over the last ten years, but they didn't reply.

I had a telephone call from the man who'd sent the letter. I explained that if I had written a disallowed prescription, which I hadn't, we would have paid for it anyway. This would have meant that it wouldn't have cost the National Health Service any money, so in actual fact the N.H.S. would have benefited from it. He replied, 'Oh, no. It's not just a question of that. We could have you before a committee and fine you as well.'

I could hardly believe it. My flurry of correspondence did mean that I received a letter from one up the scale, the Deputy Administrator for the area, who said that he wanted to emphasise the action taken was decided not by non-medical people employed by the F.P.C., but by the Special Reference Panel which is composed of a lay Chairman of the F.P.C. and two medical members, one of whom is also Secretary of the local Medical Committee.

So we have now reached a stage in general practice where we cannot prescribe what we like. If we stray from the government list we have to pay for the medicine that we've prescribed; in addition to that we can be fined for actually so doing. George Orwell *was* right.

I couldn't believe that this situation existed, other than perhaps in the armed forces. I was surprised that my colleagues in the British Medical Association and the College of General Practitioners had not made more of a fight of it. I thought it was an appalling state of affairs which sadly was destroying the

relationship between general practitioners and the F.P.C. which had always been good, and would surely drive doctors towards private medicine.

I think this is all so sad. In spite of its faults, the benefits of the National Health Service far outweigh its deficits. But letters like the one I received and rules like this one would surely destroy it. If nobody else was going to fight, I was determined to, at least until they carried me away kicking and screaming.

CHAPTER 17

Lucky Dip

Pam and I were never great takers of photographs; we always relied on people taking photographs of us. But over the years we'd somehow collected a mass of transparencies and photos of various holidays. They weren't properly filed or in order or even labelled.

Occasionally we'd have an evening when we'd bring a huge box of assorted slides down and pop them in the projector. It was like taking a lucky dip. The unexpected and sometimes long-forgotten pictures would bring memories flooding back of holidays with the children.

A lovely photo of the three children sitting on the bonnet of an old Ford Zephyr when their ages must have ranged from three to 13, with Pam and I loading luggage on the roof: a well-composed photo which had been taken by a professional. At the time I was writing for *Mother* magazine and all the contributors had to write about their holidays.

This holiday was a camping one in Brittany. We were met at the ferry by a photographer from the magazine who photographed us on the quay, all over the ship, just about everywhere you could think of. All the other passengers thought we were visiting celebrities.

Camping in Brittany was memorable. I'd left the *carnet* – camping permit – at Carnac. Having set up our tents at Penvins in a storm, I had to journey back to pick up the *carnet* otherwise we'd be thrown off the campsite.

Trevor came into his own while I was away, holding the tent down while the storm did its best to uproot it. Father eventually got back to add his weight to the bottom of the tent, and we finally managed to tether the brute securely.

There were transparencies of a holiday with our widowed friend, Margaret Doe, and her daughter Sally. We'd rented a flat for three weeks in Loano, a seaside resort near the French border in Italy. Seven of us were packed in a Ford Zephyr with food for a month – mainly tinned ham – and camping equipment piled high on the roof rack. The car was so heavily-laden I daren't stop suddenly.

We got caught up in traffic on the motorway outside Versailles. Everybody was going at 70, even in the slowest lane,

and lorries were steaming past us at about 100 miles an hour. It was a nightmare. I eventually got off the motorway, and was going down a secondary road, when somebody shot out of a side road. I slammed on the brakes and the whole of the roof rack shot forward about four feet.

I managed to fix the roof rack, using the whole of my mechanical equipment – a pair of pliers, a spanner and a screwdriver – and we made our objective for our first day: Chalon-sur-Saône, about 350 miles from Le Havre.

In those days when we crossed the Channel we used to take the night boat to Le Havre with the mistaken idea that arriving in France at seven o'clock in the morning would leave us fresh for the drive south.

The boats were always crammed. Every cabin (which we couldn't afford anyway), and every reclining seat had been booked months ago. We had to find a bit of floor space to lie down or try and sleep in the car.

What it really meant was that we arrived in France in the small hours, having missed a night's sleep with a 350-mile car journey ahead of us.

From Le Havre we had pressed on and on without a stop, happy to be introducing Margaret and Sally to France for the first time and telling wonderful tales of French bread and cheese and pâté. When we'd just about reached exhaustion we started looking for some refreshment, but we seemed to have come to a part of the country that did not in any way cater for motorists.

Eventually we found a little cafe sign. A very strange woman answered the door, and we asked for bread and cheese.

'Toasted?' she said.

This didn't sound very French, but we agreed.

Five minutes later she brought out pieces of typical sliced English soggy bread, toasted and covered with packet cheese – not quite what we'd had in mind. After my public relations job on the delights of simple French food, the toasted cheese *à l'Anglais* must have been a big disappointment for Margaret and Sally.

We made a good campsite at Chalon-sur-Saône and had quite a nice drive the next day to a campsite by a lake near the Swiss border. From the camping book, it appeared to be a really good site, but it was in fact awful. The lake was covered in scum, there was hardly room to stand up between the tents, and the toilets ran even the Moroccan toilets a close second. You were a brave man if you didn't wear wellingtons when you set off for your daily ablutions.

We then had the most beautiful drive through the Jura Mountains and over the Mount Cenus Pass into Italy, a hair-raising experience in our heavily-laden car.

We found a lovely little Italian hilltop campsite on green grass, with good toilets, a water supply, and a glorious view over hilly countryside.

Driving in Italy seemed different, and I never got quite used to it. Outside Turin we got on to the autoroute and, although I quite enjoy driving on the right-hand side of the road, I forgot that the left-hand side was the fast lane. Having got in the fast lane I had the nightmare of trying to creep across to the slow one with every horn in Italy blaring at me.

We also took a wrong turning off the autoroute; instead of bypassing Turin we managed to go right through the centre in the rush hour. Although parts of the town were beautiful, we went through some pretty mangy, sordid areas. I just hoped the car wouldn't break down. I thought it was never going to end, but we eventually got through it and caught sight of the Mediterranean.

We tracked down our flat in Loano and I felt very much 'mission accomplished'. I settled down with a glass of wine and a large cigar – it was in the days when I was a smoker – and let the rest of the team do the unpacking.

It's a holiday Pam won't forget. She went off one afternoon to have her hair done, and came back looking very glamorous.

She sat on the beach a little off from us, reading. A nondescript Italian gentleman of middle age sidled up to her.

We all watched from about 20 yards away. Pam read on unconcernedly as he gently edged towards her. He got almost to within touching distance, then started to pick up handfuls of sand and trickle it over her feet.

This was too much for the kids. Jane shouted, 'What's that man doing to my mummy?' The startled Italian turned round, saw the watching gallery and shot off down the beach. Pam preened herself that she'd had an admirer, even though he was a fairly tatty one.

It was also a holiday Paul won't forget. We all did everything together but we felt one night that the adults should go out for a meal. We counted Sally as an adult – she was 17 and just about to take 'A' Levels. As there was an Italian family in the apartment below us, we thought that Trevor, at 13, Paul, ten, and Jane, three could be safely left.

However, at one point in the evening, Paul thought he heard ghosts. Trevor was unable to reassure him, so Paul set off into the night, wandering through the town trying to find us.

He had great difficulty, but eventually found the restaurant we were in. He stood looking at us through the window, felt that he would be disturbing us if he came in, then found his way back through the dark streets, getting lost about three times before he arrived back at the flat.

He stayed awake, fully dressed, until we came back and burst into tears when we came in – worried that we would be cross with him for having gone out.

Next day he appeared to be fully recovered and was rushing up and down the beach with a football. But we can never properly see into our children's minds and never quite know what torments they are going through.

The holiday had a grand climax. We'd got a little bit tired of our flat before the end and left it early to go to a campsite we knew at Agay, in France.

This is a beautiful campsite, set among pine trees down by the sea's edge, with a marvellous restaurant, bar, good showers and toilets, as well as a good shop. It is halfway between St.

Raphael and Cannes and not too far from our friends, Jane and
Peter Churchill, who lived at Grasse.

Peter had played a very senior part in the Resistance in that
area during the war.

We rang to find out if there was a chance of them coming to
see us, and discovered that mutual friends had already rung
them to say that we were in the vicinity. They'd got hold of a
farmhouse across the road for us, said Peter, and we must go
and stay there.

The next day we went to this most beautiful farmhouse
whose doors opened with great big iron keys at least two feet
long. The farmhouse had lovely verandahs, gardens with fruit

of every imaginable type, comfortable beds, bathrooms and showers: a veritable seventh heaven.

Peter and Jane used to keep an eye on it for friends while they were away and had the use of it for their friends when necessary. It was so lovely we decided to stay an extra day and make it a hard journey on the way back.

We invited Peter and Jane for a traditional English meal, and went to the supermarket for a piece of beef. Our idea was that we should give them roast beef, Yorkshire pudding and potatoes. But the French oven in the farmhouse had a mind of its own and refused to cook it properly. The meal was a disaster.

Sadly, Peter died a few years later, but Jane recently said that they'd often had a laugh over the English roast beef that we'd tried to prepare for them.

It meant a very early start on our last day to reach Moulins and the municipal campsite in the middle of a stadium. We camped there, and made another early start the next morning, to reach Le Havre comfortably for an evening ferry. It was a hot and sticky journey. Trevor, Sally and myself were on the front seat; Margaret, Pam, Paul and Jane were on the back, mixed up with masses of shoes, thermos flasks and all sorts of bits and pieces. At one stage it was so hot that Trevor and Sally stuck together.

*   *   *

I think there was something about preparing meals for Peter and Jane that brought out the gremlins. Jane's brother lived in Tadchester and they often came to visit him. One night I was cook for a special dinner in their honour.

I bought the very best steak, chopped it and fried it, then started to casserole it with tomatoes, onions and various other things.

Pam's contribution to the cooking was masterful. 'You'll need some paprika,' she said. 'I'll put it in for you.'

Peter and Jane were arriving in half an hour. The food smelled gorgeous and was cooking beautifully. I took a sip of gravy from my ladle as I gently stirred it. The taste was magnificent.

Then there was an after taste – so hot and strong it nearly blew the back of my head off.

I couldn't understand it. I thought I'd try it on the children. They each in turn said 'That's marvellous, Dad,' and then clutched their heads as if hit by an explosion before they'd completed their sentence.

Pam was weeping.

'I'd swear,' she said, 'I only put a teaspoonful of paprika in it.'

I took the meat out and washed it under the tap. Luckily there was some aromatic liquid I'd taken out of the casserole before the disaster, so I re-cooked the meat in that, as best I could, before our guests arrived.

Although I'd taken a bit of the bite out of it, I had to fill Peter and Jane with large quantities of gin before I offered my spoilt meal. It went down very well in fact. Peter, who said he'd been having indigestion for years, was temporarily relieved of this complaint by my magic medication.

So, in the end, the meal was enjoyed and the evening went off successfully. But it always did when Peter was around. 'There's a party wherever he goes,' said Jane.

Peter told me once that he'd been in solitary confinement in a

German prisoner-of-war camp for a year. He swore that if and when he got out, he would live to the full every day that remained to him – which he did.

A few days after our paprika episode I was writing to some friends in America. Among other things, I was telling them about the dish that I'd spent a day labouring over. I shouted out to Pam. 'How do you spell paprika?' She came down with two identical cardboard drums in her hand, one with *Paprika* written on it – and the other with *Cayenne Pepper*. That was the answer – she'd put Cayenne pepper in my beautiful beef Stroganoff instead of paprika. No wonder it would blow the back of your head off.

*   *   *

We still have our treasure chest of some hundreds of unsorted slides and photos and on the odd quiet evening we dip into it, bringing back memories of holidays with the children, with each memory bringing back other memories.

Soon the whole cycle will be repeating itself. Daisy May and Paul and Gill are coming to France with us next year. We'll be taking plenty of pictures . . . and leaving Paul, Gill and Daisy May with the memories.

CHAPTER 18

On the Move

I was approaching my 60th birthday! Where had all those years gone?

Pam and I had decided that I would retire from general practice when I reached 60. This was the earliest I could get a pension, although it would be a reduced pension and there would be a pulling in of financial reins unless my writing unexpectedly took off.

As well as having reached the age that I could retire, I felt there were certain indications that were pointing in that direction.

I'd been in practice for 33 years and I kidded myself that the part of my brain which held patients' names had got full up.

I was always forgetting people's names. I could remember where they lived, where they'd been on holiday, their house, their car, the name of their dog but, so often their names escaped me.

When I was doing a surgery there was always a pile of notes in front of me in the order that the patients came in. If the patients had come in in the wrong order, there had been times when I had picked up the wrong card and had a long conversation about somebody else's condition.

I wore glasses for reading and close work, but had good long vision. Pam and I had taken to reading in bed before we went to sleep, and after reading I'd put my glasses down on the bedside table.

I had an urgent call one night – somebody desperately short of breath. I got dressed as quickly as I could and drove out four miles to Farmer Leach's farm, where I was told he was having breathing difficulties.

The Leaches had a large family in residence. There was Grandma Leach of 85, Leach himself who was about my age, four sons and three daughters, scattered round the house and in farm cottages, and about eleven grandchildren, all of them working on the farm.

I arrived, examined him, and realised he needed an intravenous injection and a pretty quick one at that – he had an acute bronchial spasm.

I put my hand in my pocket for my glasses. There was nothing there. They were still on my bedside table at home.

There was no way I could drive four miles back and pick up my glasses. Mr Leach needed an injection straight away. I had to ask, in despair, 'Has anybody in the house got a pair of glasses?'

Grandma Leach had – and Grandma's glasses improved my vision enough to get a needle into a vein.

The injection relieved Farmer Leach's breathing and all was well.

I made a vow to keep a spare pair of glasses in my case from then on. And I realised that my eyesight – let alone my memory – was no longer what it was.

At coffee time the next morning in the surgery, I regaled my partners with my experience of the previous night. They offered all sorts of helpful advice, such as tying my glasses to my head.

At evening surgery, there on my desk was a muddy sort of jam jar containing what looked like great black slugs.

Ron Dickinson came in; apparently he'd gone to great lengths to get these specimens for me. 'Not the same leech as you saw last night, Bob,' he said. 'But you don't need glasses for these to get blood – just stick them on anywhere and they'll get it for you.'

There happened to be a rolled up *British Medical Journal* on

the corner of my desk. I picked it up and threw it at him, catching him squarely on the head as he shot out of the door.

'You'll be old yourself one day!' I shouted after him. 'Come back and pick up these wobbly black puddings or I'll let them loose in your car!'

Knowing that in a few months' time I would no longer be doing night and weekend work, every night and weekend seemed to be that much harder. I was convinced that getting up at three in the morning on night calls was not doing me a lot of good. Night calls were usually for desperate situations – children fighting for breath, heart attacks, all sorts of traumatic things. Whenever I went out, my own heart seemed to be in my mouth before I started. I felt that perhaps I'd worked at this pace for long enough.

Also, although we loved Tadchester and all its surroundings, our children had gone away. Trevor and Jane were in Brighton; Paul and Gill in Cirencester. Because of the distances we saw very much less of them.

I read a book once where the author said that you should start planning your retirement when you're 40, i.e. put roots down somewhere and start getting to know the people in a particular area.

We had so often seen people retiring to Tadchester with dreams of a little cottage in the West of England, only to arrive there to find they knew no one, and were faced with the fact that in advancing years it's more difficult to strike up new relationships. They spent the last years of their lives lonely, depending on occasional visits from relatives and children and never really settling in the new community. They would have been much better off retiring in their work surroundings.

Although we hadn't started planning at the age of 40, we had always loved the Thames Valley, particularly the town of Wallingford. Over the years, with boating holidays, we had made friends there. Every time we moored at Wallingford we tramped around having a look at houses. Several times we very nearly put money down on cottages, but things had fallen through at the last minute.

With retirement only about six months off, we had to go into the business more thoroughly, and Pam used to make house-hunting trips to Wallingford. Having nearly bought one house, waiting for a completion date with still a few enquiries to be cleared, we thought we'd better keep our options open and while we were up there see what else was on the market.

Suddenly we found the house of our dreams, a house much smaller than the one we'd had in Tadchester, but big enough for Pam and me. It was within walking distance of the town centre and above all, had a lawn that went down to the river, with a mooring stage for a boat at the bottom.

We bought it on the spot.

For the next few months Pam was commuting up and down from Tadchester to Wallingford. Fortunately the house was in such immaculate condition that we had no decorating to do. Pam had half-moved in there about four months before I actually retired.

While she was away I stayed with a marvellous lady who used to put up the locums and junior partners, Mrs Doris Lounger. David Lichen, our new partner, had been staying with her while he was looking for a new house and I noticed that he had grown steadily stouter as the weeks went by.

I can't think of anybody less appropriately named than Mrs Lounger, a widow who had been a doctor's receptionist. Now, as well as putting up various locums, partners and people like myself, she had a morning job cleaning cars for a garage. Her work was immaculate: a car cleaned by Mrs Lounger would put about £500 on its price.

She utterly spoiled me and any of my colleagues who stayed with her. She was up and about at six every morning, cleaned my car windows and went down to the shop for a paper. So by the time I got up at about eight o'clock, breakfast was ready, my paper was there and my car was cleaned.

Her evening meals were of cordon bleu standard. And we had a common weakness – egg and chips was our favourite dish. On high days and holidays she would say with a twinkle in her eye, 'Guess what's for supper tonight?' Yes, it would be egg and chips and we would blissfully dip our chips in the yolk.

Years ago, Doris had been the head cook in a large house. It was back in the days of Upstairs and Downstairs, and she still maintained the standards of the landed gentry. She was a wonderful little woman and marvellous company.

She had a very old cat called Tommy, whose ginger hairs seemed to stick to every piece of clothing I wore. They could only be cleared by wrapping a band of Sellotape sticky side up round my fingers and dabbing it on to pick off the hairs. A small price to pay for such wonderful hospitality.

Mrs Lounger's daughter had gone to New Zealand some years before. As she had other children, she was unable to spend longer than six months at a time on her visits there. So she saved for her New Zealand trips and in the meantime kept an immaculate house and garden, ran around in a small car, cleaned cars and cared for us all splendidly.

The last few months before retirement were very emotional. I'd been in Tadchester for such a great number of years that inevitably I'd become part of people's lives. Now I was deserting them. There was party after party, magnificent presents including a pine table, benches and chairs – it seemed like about ten Christmases all rolled into one. We had a formal practice dinner where we all wore dinner jackets and made speeches and wondered why we had never done this before. I was presented with a pair of silver candlesticks and a beautiful watercolour painting.

Not only was I going to miss my partners, who were really like family, but all the wonderful assortment of characters who'd let me into and shared part of their lives with me.

Tadchester was a wonderful little town and a wonderful little community. I was going to miss it terribly. But I was missing my children more and, with Wallingford being fairly near to London, we knew we wouldn't be short of visitors.

Before I left Tadchester we'd already got our eye on river holidays and had purchased an old hire boat from a neighbouring boatyard. The boat had the luxury of a flush toilet, shower, hot and cold water, a fridge and a gas oven.

No more ablutions under an umbrella in the corner of a field in the pouring rain.

I was in that catch-22 situation, I couldn't bear to leave Tadchester and I couldn't wait to get to Wallingford.

We cleared up the house in Tadchester, which was bought by a pleasant young couple with two small children, and had our last round of goodbyes to friends and patients.

The farewell to the practice staff was held on a Friday lunchtime in the Surgery. I was actually to finish work on the following Sunday, when I would be going round with the new young partner who was to replace me. Pam and I had decided to drive through the Sunday night to arrive at our new house, to begin our new life at the start of a new day.

I had thought the staff goodbye party was muted, perhaps because we were all so upset about parting. But apart from that, it seemed that they hadn't taken quite as much trouble as they usually did when one of their own colleagues left. Anyway it was all very nice, with lots of kisses, lots of photographs taken. We went easy on the drink as we all had to work in the afternoon.

Saturday on duty was an anticlimax; not many calls, an appendicitis I had to send to hospital at 1 a.m. I hoped it would be my last night call ever.

159

There were only two calls on Sunday morning, so I sat with Pam reading the papers, waiting for the new young partner to arrive. We were staying at Mrs Lounger's and my replacement was expected at lunchtime. There was something strange about the morning. Mrs Lounger seemed to have lost the usual bustle associated with one of her Sunday lunches. Pam seemed ill at ease. Then, just as the new young partner arrived, there came an emergency call: would I go immediately to a visitor with chest pain who was staying in the house next door to Anne Matthews, one of our receptionists? The new partner offered to go but I felt I ought to see the job through. I shot off in my car with my heart in my mouth as usual, wondering what crisis I would have to deal with.

I tore up the muddy lane that led to Anne Matthews' lovely half-timbered country house. Standing in the middle of the road was David Lichen, directing me into Anne Matthews' drive, 'God,' I thought. 'They have sent for him as well.'

I turned into Anne's drive, noticing about 40 cars parked in the field behind the house. When I turned the corner, there were about 50 people, all with filled glasses raised to me. I could see all the Surgery staff and their husbands, my partners, health visitors, district nurses, old locums – everybody I had worked with at Tadchester over the years. This was my real goodbye party and it was almost too much. Mrs Lounger and Pam arrived about five minutes later. They, the devils, had been in on the secret all the time.

We had a marvellous party on a lovely summer's day in the magnificent setting of the Matthews' old country house on a hilltop, with a panoramic view of the whole of Tadchester. I shall never forget it. I was given a longitudinal map of the Thames that I had always wanted, an inscribed barometer for my boat from the Surgery girls, and a pair of binoculars.

They had really spoilt me, and made my last view of Tadchester such a beautiful one.

The party went on until the evening. Then it was back to Mrs Lounger's for reviving coffee, talk until the early hours and final goodbyes. We set off, aiming to arrive in Wallingford as near dawn as possible.

Our hearts were very heavy, but our spirits were high. Dawn rose as we reached Pangbourne and for the last few miles we were able to see stretches of the Thames.

Just before we entered Wallingford we turned down into a small cul-de-sac of half a dozen houses, all with lawns stretching down to the river. We went into our new house and climbed up into the bedroom which had a balcony overlooking the river.

The sun was now shining, it was a lovely day. A neighbour had cut the grass down to the river's edge and there bouncing on its moorings was our new boat *Sea Grey*. It all looked so beautiful.

I turned to Pam. She smiled. 'I know what you're going to say.'

'Yes,' I said. 'Life is going to be different from now on.'

Postscript

There is the fable of the old man sitting outside a town, being approached by a stranger.

'What are they like in this town?' asked the stranger.

'What were they like in your last town?' replied the old man.

'They were delightful people. I was very happy there. They were kind, generous and would always help you in trouble.'

'You will find them very much like that in this town.'

The old man was approached by another stranger.

'What are the people like in this town?' asked the second stranger.

'What were they like in your last town?' replied the old man.

'It was an awful place. They were mean, unkind and nobody would ever help anybody.'

'I am afraid you will find it very much the same here,' said the old man.

If it should be your lot to ever visit Tadchester, this is how you will find it.